Souness

The Management Years

Souness

The Management Years

Graeme Souness with Mike Ellis

André Deutsch

First published in 1999 by
André Deutsch Ltd
76 Dean Street
London W1V 5HA
www.vci.co.uk

A catalogue record for this book is available from the British
Library

ISBN 0 233 99738 5

Typeset by
Derek Doyle & Associates, Liverpool
Printed and bound in Great Britain by
MPG Books, Bodmin, Cornwall

1 3 5 7 9 10 8 6 4 2

Front jacket photograph by Roger Dixon
Back jacket photograph © Mirror Syndication International
Jacket and plate section designed by Design 23

Acknowledgements

Mike Ellis, who collaborated with Graeme Souness in the writing of this book, has covered soccer on Merseyside for 35 years. Born in Rhyl, he entered journalism on a local weekly newspaper after leaving school. Called up for National Service at 18, he spent 19 months in Cyprus before resuming his career with the *Northern Daily Mail* in Hartlepool. In 1963 he joined the *Daily Herald* sports staff in Manchester before becoming the paper's man on Merseyside.

He has written for the *Sun* since its launch in October 1969. He covered Liverpool's first game in Europe in 1964 and their most recent in 1998. He has witnessed all the highs and lows of the club during that period, including the four European Cup successes and the tragedies of Heysel and Hillsborough.

Apart from reporting on Liverpool and Everton, he has also covered international football with Wales, Northern Ireland and the Republic of Ireland.

Married with two children, he lives in Cheshire.

Contents

Foreword

by David Murray, Chairman,
Glasgow Rangers FC

The first time I met Graeme Souness I knew he was a man of conviction and substance. Rangers needed somebody like him to turn around an ailing club and that is exactly what he did.

His contribution to restoring Rangers as Scotland's number one club cannot be over-emphasised after they had spent so many years in the shadow of Celtic.

Graeme is an acquired taste and not everyone's cup of tea but wherever he goes he will be a winner and his track record in management proves that. In many respects he is a misunderstood individual. He has made some enemies in the game but he has always remained true to his principles. At Rangers he would never allow anything to stand in his way when he began his task and we have enjoyed the benefits ever since.

Along the way we became close friends as well as business associates devoted to reviving the club. We both quickly realised there was a line that could not be crossed in our different roles as chairman and manager. But we always had the same aim – we wanted to be winners and we wanted Rangers to succeed. Sometimes I would take the initiative, on other occasions it would be Graeme, but we knew whoever took the lead we could trust and rely on each other for complete support.

As a chairman I have always worked on the principle that I am on the same side as the manager and we should both be striving for the same goals. Graeme and I come from different backgrounds but we are of a similar age and we shared the same determination to make Rangers great again. Graeme can be fiery, yet I can honestly say we never fell out at any stage during our working relationship. The ground rules established then have remained in place during my association with Walter Smith and now Dick Advocaat.

Every manager has highs and lows in his career but Graeme's record shows he is well in credit when you consider the trophies he has won at different clubs. We spent a lot of time in each other's company and socialised on a regular basis. His family are personal friends of mine and we have never lost touch since he left Rangers. It is true I told him he would regret returning to Liverpool but once his mind is made up he can be very stubborn. That stems from a belief that he must do what his mind dictates. It was not a smartarse remark by me but I know he has never forgotten it.

I made it because I knew he was under a misapprehension that he was going back to a club where he had enjoyed so much success as a player and thought that everything would be the same. I knew he was going back to a different Liverpool and I wanted him to realise how much he was sacrificing by leaving Rangers.

I take no pleasure from the problems he encountered at Liverpool and I have absolutely no doubt he will return to the game at some stage and wherever that might be, he will make things happen.

Football introduced us to each other and I am grateful for

that. But the friendship it forged takes precedence over everything else. He is a man's man and I am proud to know him.

David Murray, July 1999

Introduction

It was always my intention to write a book about my experiences in soccer management. I wanted my version of my career to be honest and accurate, and I apologise if I have reopened some old wounds along the way.

I have to live with the general opinion that in most people's eyes on Merseyside I failed as manager of Liverpool. In this book I have given my account of what happened during my time at Anfield. It can be argued that I should have presented my side of the story years ago, but I was reluctant to revive painful memories for the families who lost loved ones at Hillsborough in 1989. It is not easy to talk about those events but I do feel I have an obligation to say something after unwittingly contributing to their heartache.

I don't know how they perceive me but I do know I owe them a genuine apology. It was never my intention to cause them any offence but I realise it happened and I have to accept that. I find it very difficult to put myself in their shoes and I don't know how I would have coped if the Hillsborough disaster had affected my family.

I can only offer a truthful account of my involvement. Perhaps I should have had a better grasp of the situation on Merseyside in the wake of that dreadful event, but I was working in Scotland at the time and was unaware of the depth of feeling in Liverpool. Through my ignorance I unintentionally contributed to the despair of those who lost loved ones, and it tainted my reputation in their eyes.

When I agreed to write an exclusive story for the *Sun* about my heart operation, which was three years after Hillsborough, I invited my enemies to have a field-day at my expense. For the record, once I realised how much damage that article had caused I never accepted a penny and the only beneficiary was a children's hospital in Liverpool.

It did not make any difference to my critics. They never allowed me to forget what was an error of judgement; they latched on to it and never let go. They used it to hammer me in my last two seasons as manager at Liverpool and when we failed to capitalise on the 1992 Cup Final success they had an extra string to their bow.

When you are in the public domain your mistakes leave you wide open to attack. But I do wonder how I have managed to be portrayed as such a cold, uncaring type of person. Even today there are references to the tea cup throwing incident which happened during a cup tie at Bolton in 1993. Yes it did happen, but it was the exception to the rule. It was sufficient for my critics to paint a picture of some Scottish tyrant rampaging through the dressing room attempting to impose an atmosphere of intimidation and fear. Is that really how people see me? Surely not. I may have been a menacing figure on the pitch, but off it I have always tried to conduct myself in a proper and civilised manner. I like to think I am polite in the company of strangers. I don't seek confrontation and have many interests away from the game. I love spending time in my garden. I like to travel and have been fortunate enough to visit many exciting places around the world. I make no apology for enjoying the good things in life. I take pleasure from eating out in top restaurants and I think I know a little about the wine trade. But these are minor vices in my opinion.

But the problem with my so-called image remains. Yes, I was too hard on the players at Rangers and Liverpool but you can put that down to my inexperience as a manager at the time. I don't consider myself a ruthless individual – anything but. People who know me will say I can be a soft touch and I don't mind that either. But you acquire a label in football and it is very difficult to change public perception of you as an individual. In my experience many of the players who earned reputations on the pitch were very different when they came off it. The same applies to managers who might be caught screaming and shouting on the touchline. Remember, most of us are family men with children and wives to go home to. I have a better balance to my life now. I had to change, otherwise the game would have literally killed me. I knew that when there was a real doubt whether I would come through my heart bypass operation. I vowed there and then that if I did survive I would change a few things.

Meeting Karen was a watershed in my life. It happened at a particularly traumatic time for me and if people do notice a change in my demeanour they can put it down to Karen. We first met only weeks before I discovered the seriousness of my heart condition but throughout all my trials and tribulations since, Karen has been by my side. She has needed to be my prop and support in difficult times and I cannot emphasise too much the effect she has had on me.

We are a big family. Between us Karen and I have six children with our recent arrival. I joke about it, saying if I ever come back in another world I would want it, to be as a player rather than a manager, because with all those school fees mounting up I would need the huge salaries which are on offer in the Premiership these days!

From a personal point of view, I have always carried a great guilt with me that I have not always been there for my children. I came from a stable family background. My mother and father were always there for me and my two brothers when we were growing up in Edinburgh. When my first marriage broke up one of the most difficult tasks I had was to say goodbye to my son Jordan at Edinburgh airport when he was leaving to live in Majorca with his mother. He was only three years of age and I won't forget the look in his eyes when he asked me when he would see me again. When a marriage fails there are always two sides to the story. No doubt my first wife has her version and I have mine but I shall always be responsible for my children. Constantly I wonder if I could have been a better father to them. I worry in case it has any effect on them, because I only knew the security of a strong household when I was growing up. I am in regular contact with them and we all see each other often, but I carry this guilt with me that perhaps I should have done more for them.

I am proud of my achievements as a player and a manager. It did not work out at Liverpool and that is a genuine regret but I can assure you it was not for the want of trying.

History will show I have been a successful manager so far. I won trophies at Rangers, Liverpool and Galatasaray. I kept Southampton in the Premiership and took Benfica from eighth in the table to runners-up with a place in the Champions League in my first season in Portugal. But I shall always be branded a failure as Liverpool manager. I think what has happened to them since reinforces my argument that they were in decline before I took charge. It hurts me because it is Liverpool – once the best club in Europe. I take no pleasure from their current predicament but I will argue with anyone who tries to place all the blame at my door. In football it is too simplistic to say, 'change the manager and everything will be OK'. It does not work like that. If it did every team in the land would be successful in next to no time. I don't know Gerard Houllier but I hope he is given the time to revive them. He faces a similar predicament to the one I inherited. Some of his players are not good enough and he is looking for instant replacements. It can be a high-risk business but just as I had no alternative so he must back his judgement. I take no pleasure from seeing Manchester United and Arsenal dominate English football. When I think of Liverpool I like to remember the good years – even if that seems a bygone age now.

My biggest enjoyment in football today is to be out on the training ground working with players. The hardest part is dealing with those who think they are superstars and expect to be treated as such off the pitch. I played with some great players and I know the difference between some of today's high-profile performers and the genuine article. Better players than me have not been successful in management and I just wonder if they got frustrated because they were dealing with big names who simply did not justify their standing in the game. I remember Martin Buchan quickly coming to the conclusion that management was not for him when he stopped playing at Manchester United and tried the other side of the business at Burnley. Bobby Charlton and Bobby Moore did not last long either at Preston and Southend respectively and there are other truly great players who decided that management was not for them. I can understand why.

If nothing else I hope this book clarifies a few points and enables people to have a clearer understanding of what makes me tick. I don't expect to change or influence some people who already have their ideas set in stone but this is my honest version of events and whether they agree or not is irrelevant. Other people have written books about me and some of their observations came as a big surprise. It feels odd reading detailed accounts of your life written by people you have never actually met. I suppose there is an amusing side to that, but this is my account, designed to put the record straight – mistakes and all.

Football and a great personal tragedy became intertwined at Hillsborough and I became a central figure in it although it was by accident rather than design. I would love to turn the clock back but life is not as simple as that. I have an unusual surname and I am proud of it. There is only one Souness in football and I accept if it ever crops up as a topic of conversation with most Liverpool fans the comments will not be complimentary. Maybe one time they thought I was a decent player for their club but other events have since taken precedence.

Hindsight is a wonderful thing. They say you should never go back and I should have listened to David Murray, the Rangers chairman, when he said I would regret returning to Liverpool. Of course I have made mistakes but I am who I am and that is the way it is. Show me a person who claims never to have made a mistake and I will show you a liar. Whatever my shortcomings at least I am prepared to admit them.

As a player I knew I made some enemies and I took that for granted. My style of play invited confrontation. I was hard but my philosophy was that every game was there to be won. If you did not give everything for the cause it was a pointless exercise going on to the pitch in the first place. There is an old saying, 'Those who live by the sword die by the sword' and there were a few characters with long memories hoping to exact revenge on me at some stage. Even when I retired as a player I needed to keep my wits about me when

I turned out in testimonial games. In the end I decided not to play in any more because I remained a marked man even on those occasions. I made one exception for Ray Kennedy.

He was a fine player and a friend of mine when we were together at Liverpool and to be struck down with Parkinson's disease at such a young age was a tragic blow. Liverpool and Arsenal staged a game for him at Highbury on 27 April 1991, when I was still managing Rangers. That was one match I was determined not to miss and it is a measure of the respect Ray commanded at both clubs that so many other old friends made sure they were there for him.

Ray Clemence was working for Spurs and had a reserve game to attend earlier in the day of the testimonial. He explained his problem to the organisers but he raced to Highbury after the Spurs game and took over from Bruce Grobbelaar at half time. That was typical of the response – everyone who knew Ray wanted to do their bit to help. Kenny Dalglish played, so did Jimmy Case – Ray's closest pal at Anfield – plus other established Liverpool players such as Jan Molby, Peter Beardsley, Steve Nicol and Ray Houghton. It was a reminder of the good old days when Liverpool bonded as a team. Tony Adams, Nigel Winterburn, Kevin Campbell, David Rocastle and Michael Thomas – later to join Liverpool – were in the Arsenal ranks.

I remember that occasion because it was a throwback to the Liverpool team of the 1980s. We were all obsessed with winning in those days. As a player I was single-minded, loyal to the club and 100 per cent committed. I earned a few admirers along the way because the fans knew what to expect when I was on the pitch. I never claimed to be the greatest, or to possess the skill of a Kenny Dalglish, but I was always ready to fight for the cause. As a player I did not really care what people thought about me. I was a working-class lad and I had fought my way up the ladder of professional football.

Some of my colleagues dubbed me 'Champagne Charlie' but I never forgot where I came from and my roots remained firmly in Edinburgh. It served to rubberstamp a general perception of me. Because I was hard and uncompromising on the pitch, I am regarded as a cold, uncaring type of person but away from the football field I have always tried to conduct myself in a proper and correct manner.

1

Joining Rangers

A telephone call at the start of 1986 was to change my life and launch my managerial career at Rangers. At the time I was playing for Sampdoria and halfway through a three-year contract after joining them from Liverpool.

Ironically, the Sampdoria president had asked me just weeks before Rangers made contact if I was planning to stay in Italy and I had assured him that I was more than happy to do so. I enjoyed living in Genoa and I thought it was an ideal place to finish my playing career. Coaching and management had crossed my mind because I was into my thirties and nothing lasts for ever, but at that stage I had nothing planned after I stopped playing, although I was beginning to form my own ideas.

The World Cup in Mexico was coming up so I was anticipating a busy summer, but management was not on the cards. Never in my wildest dreams did I think a club the size of Rangers would even consider a person with no experience for such a massive job. Imagine how I felt when David Holmes contacted me out of the blue to ask if I would be interested. Interested? You bet I was.

Lawrence Marlborough was the major shareholder at Ibrox in 1986 but he was pursuing other business interests in America and David looked after his football affairs in Glasgow, as well as being chairman of Lawrence Construction in Scotland.

I met David and Rangers chairman John Payton at the Mayfair Hotel in London and was flattered they were prepared to consider somebody with no track record other than as a player. I knew I could still perform on the pitch for a couple of years but my managerial experience was nil. The prospect of taking charge certainly appealed to me but they must have realised they were taking a gamble and they were prepared to do that. It was a wonderful opportunity and I promised to get back to them after discussing it with my wife. We had moved to Italy because it was necessary for her to live outside the UK for tax reasons.

That still applied so we agreed she would join her family in Majorca and I would be on my own in Glasgow for the first 12 months. I had a second meeting in Milan with David Holmes but really it was just a formality because I had made up my mind to accept their offer, and to succeed Jock Wallace to become the first player-manager in Rangers history. David Holmes flew in and out the same day – it only took a couple of hours to finalise the agreement.

It left me in a difficult situation with Sampdoria because I had already assured them I would be staying for another season and they had plans to strengthen the team. They had some promising young players coming through – among them Gianluca Vialli, now at Chelsea – and I had told the president that if he could add some extra quality to the squad we would have a chance to challenge for the Serie A title the following season.

He was working under the impression that I would be playing and now I faced the task of explaining the new development. To make matters worse he had agreed to sell another midfield player who would have been the obvious replacement for me.

Mattioli had arrived from Como earlier in the season and the plan was for him to become my partner. It never really worked out and he complained to the president that we were too similar in style. Arrangements were made for him to move to Inter Milan because I had informed Sampdoria I would be staying. They were certainly entitled to feel aggrieved when I told them I wanted to take the Rangers job but they were really understanding and supportive. It was typical of the way I had been treated throughout my time at Sampdoria. There was no question of recriminations – instead they wished me well and gave me their blessing to move back home to Scotland at the end of the 1985–86 season.

I shall always remember that gesture because I did feel some guilt even though I had not instigated the Rangers interest. I think Sampdoria understood what it meant to me and they never placed any obstacles in my path. It is a fine club run by honourable men and I shall always be grateful for the experience of playing for them.

At that point it was essential to keep everything quiet. I had agreed to take over at Rangers after the World Cup but that was still some months away so I had promised to play out the season with Sampdoria. But I was already beginning to prepare for Ibrox.

David Holmes rightly pointed out I would need somebody with experience of the Scottish game and he suggested Walter Smith as the ideal choice to be my right-hand man. Walter was at Dundee United and although I did not know him personally, I was aware that he had an excellent reputation. My only contact with him had been at international fixtures. Jock Stein was the national coach and Walter was

11

in charge of the Under-21 team. When Jock tragically died at Ninian Park in September 1985 at the end of a qualifying match against Wales, Walter and Alex Ferguson were appointed to take the squad to Mexico for the 1986 World Cup.

Born in Glasgow, Walter was a Rangers fanatic. His dream had been to play for the club but it never materialised. Instead he carved out a solid career with Dumbarton and Dundee United before becoming Jim McLean's assistant at Tannadice. We came from similar working-class backgrounds and although I was from Edinburgh and occasionally watched Hearts as a boy I can remember going through to Ibrox on numerous occasions for the big European nights. Somehow we both managed to keep the lid on the negotiations about what was going to happen, and that was quite an achievement. In football, stories have a habit of leaking out but this one stood the test of time until Rangers were ready to make the announcement.

Walter and I met at Turnberry in February 1986 when the Scotland team was preparing for a game against Yugoslavia. That was when I asked him if he would join me at Rangers. He never hesitated and I quickly came to the conclusion that I could work with him. He was a straight-down-the-middle, honest guy who was always prepared to say his piece and his vast experience of the Scottish game was to prove invaluable to me. Now this may come as a surprise when you consider the popular image of me but we never had a cross word in five years together. We understood each other right from the start and I respected and listened to his opinions. I could not have asked for a better man to be by my side.

As the World Cup preparations began to gather pace we found ourselves in a bizarre situation. Technically he was one of my bosses in the Scotland set-up even though we both knew the roles would be reversed when we went to Ibrox. During the build-up to the World Cup we would always meet in his room to plan our campaign for Rangers. As a player I was sharing with another member of the squad and we could not take the risk of someone bursting in unexpectedly and finding the pair of us planning a totally different agenda.

Somehow the secret remained watertight until Rangers made the formal announcement in April 1986. It was a major surprise and although there were some who had reservations about giving the job to an untried candidate, the majority gave me an enthusiastic welcome.

Even then there were a few twists to the tale. I had agreed to play out the season with Sampdoria and returned to Italy for the remaining games while Walter held the fort at Ibrox. I came back to play in a testimonial at Hampden and was enormously encouraged by the response I received from the Rangers fans at the match.

Those were heady days. The World Cup was on the horizon and the Rangers job was waiting when we returned: I certainly had a special buzz in the summer of 1986.

It was really quite extraordinary that Rangers had not won the Championship since 1978. Jock Wallace did the treble that year, adding the Scottish Cup and League Cup to the title – the second time he had managed that for Rangers. This came on top of their only European success when they won the Cup-Winners' Cup in 1972. Rangers fans were entitled to believe that another golden era was being ushered in, but football is never as predictable as that. They only needed to remember a similar barren spell of 11 years without a championship before Jock delivered again in 1975.

When Jock left at the end of the 1978 season to join Leicester he was replaced by one of Ibrox's favourite sons: John Greig. John had been a key figure in the treble-winning side and he made a flying start in his new role. In John's first season, Rangers retained the two domestic Cups and also enjoyed a terrific run in the European Cup, disposing of Juventus and PSV Eindhoven before going out at the quarter-final stage to Cologne.

Celtic took the title and John was never able to reclaim it. It was not just Celtic who were a major force at the time. Dundee United were also competing for the major trophies and so were Alex Ferguson's Aberdeen.

When John resigned in 1983 Jock, who had moved on from Leicester to Motherwell, returned for his second stint at the helm. He was unable to repeat his title success during his first period in charge and left again in April 1986.

He managed Spanish club Seville, then Colchester before becoming a victim of Parkinson's disease. The illness forced him out of the game and eventually claimed his life but before that sad event he was a regular visitor to Ibrox and was always a welcome figure. I was aware of the history and tradition of Rangers and their need to become the number one club again. Very few people get the opportunity to manage a club of this size and I was very conscious of the responsibility which had been handed to me.

When I arrived at Ibrox, David Holmes played a crucial role helping me settle into my new environment. He supported me to the hilt and we had a terrific spell together. He backed me all the way and his wife, Betty, also played her part. They would go to various Rangers Supporters' Clubs throughout Scotland every week to promote a family atmosphere and spread the word that we were beginning the process of restoring the glory days. They had gone nine years without winning the championship but he reminded everyone that we were all in this together and were determined to put Rangers back on top.

When a club is successful it is always the players and the management who take the credit and it is easy to forget those who also put in so much hard work behind the scenes. I certainly won't forget the support and encouragement I received from David Holmes. He played a key role when I outlined my plans. I suppose they were considered revolutionary at the time and I knew by the look on Walter's face when he heard what I proposed to do that we were about to cause some shockwaves on the Scottish scene. I could hardly wait!

Nothing you learn as a player can prepare you for management. It is a totally different world and a huge step to take, especially when you are starting at one of the biggest clubs in Britain. It was a very proud day for me when I walked through the door at Ibrox. I realised I had been given a wonderful opportunity and I was coming home after playing all my football outside Scotland.

And it was the mighty Rangers who had presented me with this chance. I really did feel ten feet tall but not out of arrogance or conceit. You did not need to be a Rangers fan to know their history and reputation. Scotland may be a small country but the Scots' passion for football never wanes. In Glasgow it dominates the lives of most of the population because of the fierce rivalry which has always existed between Rangers and Celtic. Being a son of Edinburgh helped me because I had not been raised in the Glasgow environment which dictates you either support one club or the other. I was able to take a more detached point of view although I was totally committed to the Rangers cause. It is impossible not to be infected by the raw passion which the game generates in such a soccer-mad city. It stretches around the world. Rangers and Celtic are and always will be *the* teams in Scotland and one of them had entrusted their future to me. It was the job most footballers could only dream of yet here I was with the keys to the door and I was determined to love every minute of it.

The size of the task did not deter me because I have always had total confidence in my ability. My enemies will claim that is a weakness but I approached the job at Rangers in a positive frame of mind and I was ready to make a success of it.

Ask any player who has moved into management and I guarantee they will give you the same answer as me. Nothing prepares you for what is a step into the unknown: there is no apprenticeship and no exams to pass. A case of sink or swim. After playing for Middlesborough, Liverpool and Sampdoria I thought I had a good understanding of how a football club worked but I quickly discovered I knew only one side of it. Becoming a manager was a gigantic step.

I thought nothing of working an 18-hour day. I would be on the road until the early hours of the next morning after driving to Aberdeen, Dundee or down to England to watch players. It was a non-stop, relentless, round-the-clock schedule and I loved every minute of it. I accepted this was the life of a manager and the fact that I was also a player became incidental. I happily took on the extra workload and never looked on it as a chore. Quite the opposite, for I had the best of both worlds. I was managing a famous club with the luxury of deciding if I would play for them too.

There was a learning process to absorb but I had a clear idea in my head about which road we were going to go down. It certainly created a sensation in Scottish circles but my decision to recruit players from England seemed to be no more than common sense. Over the years the movement had always been one-way with English clubs snapping up the best players north of the border. Why not reverse the trend? I am surprised that nobody had thought of it before.

When I was a young hopeful in Edinburgh, the football drift to England was an accepted form of life. Some harboured dreams of joining Rangers or Celtic but, for most, the glamour clubs in England provided a huge attraction. Down the years a great many Scots had moved into English football and it was a proud boast that they had brought success to the likes of Manchester United, Liverpool, Arsenal and Tottenham. And nobody argued with that. Remember Dave Mackay and John White of Spurs, Billy Bremner of Leeds, Denis Law and Pat Crerand at Manchester United, Billy Liddell, Kenny Dalglish and Alan Hansen at Liverpool. Frank McLintock, George Graham and Bob Wilson maintained the Scottish tradition at Arsenal.

But when I went to Rangers, the number of Scots playing a prominent role on both sides of the border had diminished. English Clubs were looking towards Europe for new blood and the movement from Scotland had been reduced to a trickle. Sad to say, the conveyer belt of talent had dried up, which is why I had proposed that we raid England for our new recruits. I knew we would have to make it look attractive in contract terms to entice the top players to Scotland and it would be an expensive project – certainly at the beginning – but I was convinced that it would pay off in the long term.

Rangers had been in the wilderness for nine years and I knew they could not sign the best players from their own league. Celtic, Aberdeen and Dundee United would not sell to them so it was pointless dreaming about building an all-Scottish team. It was a non-starter and I recognised that immediately. There was also a problem if you recruited from abroad that remains the case today. If Rangers sign a foreign player and it does not work out there is no other market-place for him in Scotland. Rangers pay top buck for big names and the belief is if a star name cannot cut it in Scotland, his value decreases and the only alternative is to sell him back at a loss to the country where he came from. That is a recipe for financial disaster because foreign players can be so expensive. It is a similar problem with Scottish players. There is only one place for them to go if they fail elsewhere and that is to return home.

My argument was if I bought from England and the move failed it would be easier to transfer the player back to an English club without the risk of incurring such a heavy loss. It seemed a logical step but some of the Rangers board expressed surprise at the idea and were worried that the fans would resist a Sassenach invasion. I disagreed. I believed the public would welcome any new faces who would help to make Rangers the number one team again – as long as they were not Catholics!

It all began modestly enough but by the time I had finished there were squeals of anguish emanating from other Scottish managers accusing me of buying success and threatening financial disaster for the game because the transfer market was spiralling. Yes, I brought some big names to Rangers and we needed to offer attractive contracts to tempt them to join us, but my spending was modest compared to the fees which are being paid today. And at no stage during my time were we spending at the same level as the top English clubs.

And let's get it right. I had come to Rangers to be a

winner. Why should I have any sympathy with my competitors? My job was to restore Rangers to their rightful place as the top club in Scotland, and despite what some people may have thought I did not have an open cheque book to achieve that aim.

For example, my first signing cost the princely sum of £200,000. That was Colin West from Watford in May 1986, a big centre-forward with a physical presence which is essential in the Scottish game. It hardly created headline news but I was already on the trail of others who were destined to set the ball rolling in a big way for Rangers, namely Chris Woods, Terry Butcher and Graham Roberts.

It was important to cause a few ripples through England and Scotland so people would sit up and take notice. The best way to make a clear declaration of intent was to secure the services of top-line international stars who were household names north and south of the border.

I was confident I could deliver if I could tempt English-based players into Ibrox Park just to see what was on offer. The sheer size of the place and the facilities could not fail to impress anyone seeing it for the first time. I can be as persuasive as anyone and top players love to perform on a major stage. If I could convince them they would be playing in the best club stadium in Britain I was confident I could get them to sign. And I was proved right. I knew if we could make a major English signing, the word would spread that Rangers were demonstrating a dramatic shift in policy and other English players would start to take note.

The best way to influence people is by word of mouth. Players talk to each other and if I could persuade a top English star to come and play in Scotland I knew he would be my selling agent whenever he came into contact with some of his colleagues.

Better that he should extol the virtues of playing for Rangers rather than me. They would know I had a vested interest when I first spoke to them but another player could give an objective view without giving the impression he was trying to pressurise them into signing.

All that had to be conducted in the correct manner of course, and there was never any question of me using a Rangers player to make an illegal approach. I am talking about a situation when you have agreed a fee with a club and a player might be seeking assurance from somebody who had already made the move to Scotland. A variation on the domino theory: once you make the initial breakthrough, others will follow.

That was me showing a footballer's mentality. I loved to strut my stuff in front of a big crowd and I believed the same attitude will always apply to any pro worth his salt. Seducing them with the prospect of displaying their talents in a modern all-seater 45,000 capacity stadium was one of my biggest selling points when they came to Ibrox. I was not trying to con anyone. My heart was set on bringing the trophies back to Rangers and I wanted players with the same passion and belief. I was looking for leaders, strong characters who would embrace my ideals and I reckon I found a few who certainly fitted the bill.

If you want the best you must expect to pay the bill and I was always prepared to do that. Other issues were raised which never concerned me in the slightest. How would an English player react to settling in Scotland? The bottom line remains that a footballer is a footballer and moving north hardly represents a massive culture shock. I would joke with some of my English friends that they should visit Scotland more often because some of us now had colour televisions!

It never became an obstacle when I was recruiting players
– and why should it? Only those ignorant of what Scotland
has to offer as a country would reject it out of hand.

2

The English Invasion Begins

There were so many attractive areas available for my English recruits when they came to Rangers. Some settled at Helensburgh on the mouth of the Clyde which is a beautiful spot; others moved out to Dunblane in the Stirlingshire countryside and a few stayed closer to Glasgow. I always knew if I could sell them the idea of playing for Rangers there would never be a problem finding a suitable place for them to live.

I had the best of both worlds because I had the advantage of local knowledge. Call me biased if you will but I consider Edinburgh to be the most beautiful city in Britain, and that was where I intended to live when I returned. I was born there and I was thrilled to be going back. Edinburgh folk are sometimes perceived as being stand-offish but I put that down to the number of tourists who flock to the place every year. We tend to keep our distance when there are so many strangers in town.

Even Glaswegians will admit their city does not have the same appeal as the capital, particularly for visitors, but it has its own strengths. Glasgow's reputation is as a hard, working-class city and its citizens are rightly proud of that. They call a spade a spade but there is nothing wrong with that. In fact it is a more friendly place than Edinburgh, so it was never going to be a problem for my new players. All they had to do was produce on the pitch and they would be quickly adopted by the Rangers faithful. It amuses me when people who don't know the real Glasgow start sounding off about its tough image. The same things are said about Liverpool, yet both are warm, vibrant places and in next to no time you can be out of the city centre and enjoying the wide open spaces. In Glasgow's case Loch Lomond is literally just down the road.

That is why I never thought the prospect of moving north of the border would create difficulties for the players I had targeted. I was selling them my own football dream and if they didn't like the sound of that then I didn't want them on board anyway.

My first major signing was Chris Woods from Nottingham Forest in June 1986. The Liverpool team I played in was the best in Britain – I would argue it was the best in Europe – but we always struggled to beat Forest. We would blame Peter Shilton for that because we came up against him when he was at his peak, but they also had Chris Woods. In my first year at Liverpool in 1978 we played Forest in the League Cup Final. I was not eligible to play so I had a bird's-eye view of Woods at Wembley when he produced a brilliant performance in a 0–0 draw. The game went to a replay at Old Trafford when Forest proved once again to be Liverpool's bogey team by winning the trophy with a 1–0 victory.

I thought then, 'what a good young keeper you are', and I kept tabs on his progress after that. He had won his first England cap in 1984 and was considered the natural replacement for Shilton in the long term. I have always made a top keeper a priority wherever I have worked. In the games against Forest we would have 75 per cent of the play and not score simply because they had Shilton or Woods between the sticks. That taught me how important it was to have a class performer in that position and I was prepared to pay big money for the right man.

Chris cost £600,000 but it was money well spent. I wanted to build a strong backbone for my team so it made sense to start with the goalkeeper and a dominating centre-back. In my opinion Chris was the best keeper in Britain during his first two years at Rangers. A mystery virus knocked him back in his third season and there were fears for his career. His vision and balance were seriously affected but fortunately he made a complete recovery.

I had Terry Butcher in my sights while I was negotiating the Woods transfer but there were some hair-raising moments before we finally landed the man who was to play such a decisive role in the rebirth of Rangers. I remember saying to David Holmes: 'If you find me the money to sign Terry Butcher we will win the championship this year.' Manchester United and Tottenham were also on his trail so we faced serious competition and, just to complicate matters further, Terry was in Los Angeles playing for a World XI when we finally agreed a £725,000 fee with Ipswich.

It is not easy conducting a transfer with a player who is 4,000 miles away but I arranged to meet Terry at the Sheraton Hotel at Heathrow when he arrived home. It was all cloak-and-dagger stuff in case the other interested clubs were alerted that we were so close to completing the deal. When I first contacted Terry in America it was the middle of the night over there and he was a little the worse for wear after attending a function at the end of the game. Maybe he didn't understand me too clearly as I made arrangements to meet him on his return to England! We were due to meet at the Sheraton Hotel at Heathrow – the only problem was there was no sign of Terry long after the plane had landed. I hung around for ages wondering what had gone wrong before I eventually made contact with him. He had reported to the wrong hotel. Let us put it this way – Terry was feeling a little jet-lagged and emotional after his ten-hour flight! All I wanted to do was pack him on to a Glasgow-bound flight. All he wanted to do was go straight home to Ipswich and get his head down.

The last thing I needed was for Terry to sleep off his trip and possibly have second thoughts about the move the next day. By taking Terry straight to Ibrox I knew I held a trump card, once he saw the stadium and heard my plans for the future. It was essential he went to Glasgow that day, regardless of how he felt, and fortunately I managed to persuade him to do just that and he became one of the key signings in my time at Rangers. Even our fans played their part in convincing him to join us. He was worried about how he would be received in Scotland because when he came up to Glasgow to play for England he did take a lot of stick, but as the news began to leak out that he was travelling to Ibrox for talks, some of the supporters gathered outside the ground and gave him a great reception. That reinforced my argument that he would not have a problem with our fans. There was a fireplace in my office and I can remember balancing on the lip of the hearth as we discussed the transfer and I was thinking to myself 'there is no way I can let him go back to England without signing'. Terry said he wanted time to think about it and I was sticking to my guns and insisting we concluded the deal there and then. Fortunately he signed before returning home to Ipswich.

I knew what he had to offer because I had played against him on several occasions. I was looking for a leader, a real man in every sense of the word, and Butcher fitted the bill perfectly. He loved it so much in Scotland he stayed there and bought a hotel when his playing career ended. So much for the difficulties of moving to a foreign land! As a player he made an immense contribution. He got the other players organised from day one, he growled at them when it was necessary, he was perfect on the pitch and perfect off it in the PR department. He gave himself to the Rangers cause, body and soul. The club has always had a reputation for recruiting big, strong, aggressive defenders and here was the perfect example: six foot four inches of solid muscle with a fighting heart to go with it.

He was the natural choice as skipper and the rest of the lads quickly realised why. If it was not me bawling out instructions you could be sure Terry would be doing his bit to keep them on their toes. He made an instant impact, particularly in his first season after joining us in August 1986.

So I had my two key men in place for the start of my first season at Rangers, and six months later Graham Roberts arrived from Spurs for £450,000, so we had sent a strong message to Celtic and all the rest that we really did mean business. Suddenly Rangers were high-profile again. We were filling the back pages of all the newspapers and my long-awaited playing debut was also attracting considerable attention. I felt in great shape. Playing at altitude in the World Cup had honed my fitness. I had never felt better prepared for the season and I was really flying in training. I was never the quickest of players but in the weeks leading up to the big kick-off I was running away from everybody. I was on fire and I know the sight of Souness the sprinter surprised a few of my new team mates. I was in terrific nick and I knew it.

The first game could not come soon enough. Walter had tried to warn me that I would get a hot reception when I made my debut against Hibernian at Easter Road but I felt ready for anything. Not for the first time Walter was proved right. I realised that when I got my marching orders with the game just 35 minutes old. A few of the Hibs players had been waiting for this day as keenly as I had, but I was the one who became the fall guy.

My first appearance in a Rangers shirt produced all the publicity that I had been expecting, and not just in the Scottish papers. Fleet Street's finest made their way to Edinburgh for the game against Hibs and true to form I provided them with the headlines they wanted.

Obviously I can only blame myself for what happened but even as I trudged off the pitch with a red card to mark my debut I had seen enough to convince me that I had a team that was ready for the long campaign ahead.

It was to be the first of many dismissals in my two years as a player – in fact I got into more disciplinary trouble in Scotland than in all my years in England and Italy put together.

Walter had warned me what to expect. I was aware there would be a few characters in green shirts on that first day keen to make a name for themselves but, if anything, that made me more determined to get my retaliation in first! Old habits die hard. Walter had also told me about Billy Kirkwood. He was a midfield player and I knew I would be coming into direct contact with him. Walter had warned me that he was an aggressive midfield player so I went looking for him. I caught him early on and was promptly booked. After that I was waiting for him to come back at me when suddenly it all went off. I was tackled and should have gone down. Instead I stayed on my feet and staggered into a Hibs player. That provoked a major incident and players from both sides quickly became involved. George McCluskey came out of a crowd of players advancing towards me in an aggressive manner and I ran my boot up his leg. That was it – instant marching orders – and I could not complain about the decision. I was not proud of what I had done but you can not always control your basic instincts. I walked off as he was carried off.

It was the old Scottish bit. We Jocks love to think of ourselves as the underdogs and I am sure that I was a marked man as soon as I joined Rangers. The mentality was 'who the hell does he think he is? If he's coming back here to show us how to play the game we'll give him a taste of his own medicine.' But I was up for that challenge. I felt it was my duty as the boss not to duck anything. I was aware the rest of my players would be watching to see how I went about the job on the pitch and there was no way I could play a minor role in that situation. It has never been my style to back off anyway but it was then more important than ever to show that I was ready to fight the fight with the best of them.

That was my first taste of what was to come. I was a target and I got myself into more trouble throughout the season by responding to strong tackles from opponents. It was usually me who paid for it but I maintain many of those guys were trying to make a name for themselves by playing the hardman, and they should have been punished. My offence was to react when I got clattered. That incensed the crowd when we were not playing at Ibrox, and that influenced referees to make an example of me. I was getting booked and sent off when the original sinners were escaping scot-free. I would joke to Phil Boersma by saying, 'Is the target straight on the back of my shirt today?'

There was a big plus from the Hibs game which gave me an insight into the type of team I had at my disposal, and it was very encouraging. When the McCluskey incident happened every single member of my team got involved. That told me I had the players to give any side a run for their money in the chase for the title. It may sound like a strange argument, but I realised there and then I had a bunch of players who were going to stand together and that is how you build a strong unit. You need leaders and you need the rest to follow. They did that to a man at Easter Road and I knew we were on our way. This was only the start and we were by no means the finished article when it came to playing quality football but the spirit was there, the willingness to help one another, and that was a big plus to get my managerial career up and running, even if I had blotted my own copy-book.

I was determined to play as often as I could despite the suspensions which came along on a regular basis, but I began to change my mind at the start of the 1987–88 season. I thought it would be in the best interests of the team if I did not play although I still had something to offer on the pitch. There was just so much animosity being directed towards me. I was coming up to 35 and I felt my presence on the pitch was having a detrimental effect on the rest of the team because I remained public enemy number one in the eyes of the opposition.

In the end a calf injury sustained against Aberdeen that year hastened the end of my playing career. I should have come straight off when it happened but I stubbornly decided to stay on. It would be Aberdeen, wouldn't it? There was bad blood between the teams because Alex Ferguson had established them as the top dogs until we arrived on the scene and started to dominate again. Traditionally it is the 'Old

Firm' games which spark the greatest rivalry but there was also always an extra edge when we faced Aberdeen.

They had a chip on their shoulder. Alex had created a successful team and they had been top of the pile and had won a European trophy – the Cup Winners' Cup in 1983. They had been dominating the Scottish scene for a few years. Now we were on the way back – winning the title in my first year as manager – and they did not like that. Fergie was pushing the old line about the provincial team being the underdogs and we were the bigheads from Glasgow. He is a clever man and that attitude whipped up the fans as much as the players, so we always knew we would be in for a difficult time when we played them either at Ibrox or Pittodrie. There were a number of incidents in those games which made it plain they resented our new status. I should stress the injury I sustained was not the result of a malicious tackle, but another of my players, Ian Durrant, had his entire career changed in a game against Aberdeen.

The loss of Ian Durrant in October 1988 was a dreadful blow. And, of course, it had to happen against Aberdeen. Fate seemed to decree that they would be involved whenever anything controversial occurred. I felt bad about the whole business. I remember when we arrived at Pittodrie, Ian joked, 'I wonder when "Simmi" will kick me today.' He was referring to Neal Simpson who usually marked him whenever we played Aberdeen. Ian is only a little fellow but he is a bright and cute performer. He knew he was always a marked man because he had so much ability but was also mentally very sharp and had the knack of avoiding trouble. On this day he was really unlucky. Three or four players had gone for the same ball when the whistle went for an infringement. Ian took his eye off the ball and just flicked out his right leg as Simpson came in and caught him. It would never have happened if play had continued because Durrant was always too alert to fall for anything, but he was out for the rest of the season requiring a cruciate knee ligament operation. That is the one every player fears because it is career-threatening, and although he was out of the game for a long time I was delighted when he came back and even regained his place in the Scotland team after he joined Kilmarnock at the start of the 1998–99 season. To see him and Ally McCoist back in harness and enjoying an Indian summer is something that has given me untold pleasure. I'll get to 'Coisty' later on – there is certainly plenty to relate about him!

Phil Boersma, who I brought to Rangers, did a magnificent job helping Ian regain fitness. He had struck up a friendship with some of the younger players when he arrived at Rangers and Durrant was one of them. He worked around the clock with Ian. It is bad enough for a seasoned pro to sustain such a serious injury but it is even worse when it happens to somebody who has a glittering future ahead of them. Phil realised that and made sure that Ian remained positive throughout his long rehabilitation period. If you ask Durrant today I am sure he would be the first to pay tribute to Phil's role in his recovery. He was made to pound the steep steps at Ibrox and Phil was always by his side. He did extra work in the gymnasium under Phil's careful guidance to build up his strength and by the time he had finished he had a stronger and more muscular physique.

The rest of the players dubbed them 'dad and lad' because they were rarely out of each other's sight in those days. It all helped Ian – even the inevitable banter. 'Don't tackle Phil's son,' they would shout when Ian was able to join in the

training again. 'Where's your old man today?' they would
ask if Phil had been called away to attend to other duties. I
think Phil's devotion and determination to bring Durrant
through the biggest crisis of his career made a big impression on the rest of the squad. They knew they had a man
they could rely on if misfortune came their way, and it all
served to enhance Phil's reputation as an expert in his field.

Durrant was not the only one we lost that season. Chris
Woods was struck down by a virus which affected his
balance and vision, and he was unable to play for three
months, but we stayed on track for the title despite the loss
of two of our best players. If anything, the absence of
Durrant spurred us on. The little fellow was so popular with
the rest of the lads and they knew he faced the prospect of
having his knee completely rebuilt if he was going to play
again. Throughout it all he was positive and determined and
that single-minded approach helped him to relaunch his
career.

But first things first. The day I was injured stands out in
my mind for another reason. We had a winger at Rangers
named Ted McMinn and he was a real flyer. On his day he
could skin any defence and I wanted him to play in this
game. He was not sure if he could because of an injury so I
deliberately delayed his fitness test which was to be carried
out on the pitch. I wanted him to see supporters inside the
stadium before he tested his leg because I knew he would
elect to play with some encouragement from the terraces.
Yes, I was beginning learn a few of the psychological tricks
which go with management, and sure enough it only took
Ted a couple of minutes to declare himself ready and he took
his place in the team.

My problem was my own impatience. I was always in too
much of a hurry to get back playing after my injury against

Aberdeen, and I was continually breaking down because I was not prepared to allow the healing process to take its course. I should have known better at my age but Rangers always came first in my book and I was prepared to take any personal risk to keep them in the chase for honours. Eventually I paid for it but the first season went like a dream.

Celtic had won the title in the 1985–86 season under David Hay. He was a quiet person who did not seek the limelight and deliberately adopted a low profile. He was one of soccer's nice guys but very professional in the manner in which he conducted himself. He did an excellent job for Celtic but his reward was the sack when we won our first championship. Billy McNeill was brought back in his place. He did the League and Cup double when it all went wrong for us in the 1987–88 season but I believe the real reason he became Celtic manager again was to bang the drum and draw some of the attention away from us. Billy was ideal in that respect. He was comfortable in front of the television cameras and he knew the soundbites which would satisfy the media. Physically he was a big fellow and he was never afraid to say his piece. Personally I thought most of it was bluster but we are all made differently. It suited Celtic to have someone in the public eye and you cannot argue with a League and Cup double so they were entitled to believe they had made the right appointment.

From Rangers' point of view I knew there were valid reasons why we had lost the crown and I was determined it would not happen again. The record books show that the championship trophy would remain at Ibrox for the next nine years under me and Walter so Celtic paid a heavy price for that isolated success.

At the start of the 1987–88 season we were on the crest of

a wave. We were the champions, we had recaptured the imagination of the public and our attendances reflected that. From a modest 17,000 we were now attracting 40,000 gates and Ibrox was looking magnificent after all the renovation. I was convinced we could press on and set new standards in the new season. There was not a bottomless pit when it came to buying players but the arrival of Chris Woods, Terry Butcher and Graham Roberts had given us a strong base and the foundations were in place.

That trio had cost the club £1.8 million and I considered that excellent business. I was ready to play another campaign and accepted that we were not in a position to go on another spending spree immediately. I did not think it would be necessary anyway, but in football just when you think you have cracked it there is always a nasty surprise around the corner and your best laid plans can go up in smoke. It is a fact that you learn more about this game in adversity rather than when you are on a victory roll. Nobody can predict what might happen at any given stage which is what makes it such a fascinating game. But I was not thinking along those lines when Terry Butcher broke his leg early in the 1987–88 season against Aberdeen and I was also sidelined with injury against the same team.

The loss of Butcher was a dreadful blow and we never really recovered. His injury happened in an accidental clash with Alex McLeish and I knew instantly we were set for a rough ride without the big fellow at the back. At no stage had I ever taken his contribution for granted but his absence had a profound effect on our season. We fell out towards the end of his time at Rangers but that never changed my opinion of him as a man or a player. His arrival set the wheels in motion and for all the success which followed. Without him it would have taken much longer and suddenly here we were

– faced with the prospect of losing him for virtually an entire season. The best centre-back in Britain was nursing a broken leg and I knew there no were funds immediately available to replace him.

It put extra responsibility on Graham Roberts, but he was another terrific competitor and always up for the challenge. I had bought him from Tottenham midway through my first year in charge and he was an instant hit with the fans. He was another one I eventually fell out with but when you are in a tight corner and the chips are down you need players of Graham's calibre. I appointed him as skipper as soon as we lost Terry and he provided the same leadership qualities and aggressive style which has always been the Rangers trademark. Remember up in Scotland you need players who can cope with difficult pitches which would be considered substandard in England. The same applies to the grounds. Ibrox and Celtic Park are the exceptions although there have been considerable improvements at other clubs in recent years. You needed players who could ignore rough-and-ready facilities and just get on with the job. Graham came into that category; a real Rangers-type player. While Celtic was regarded as the team which could play some silky, entertaining football, at Rangers we were known as a hard team capable of grinding out results when necessary, even if it did not look particularly attractive on occasions. That is why I looked for solid, reliable characters in the mould of Butcher, Richard Gough, Terry Hurlock and Roberts. The time would come when I could add more polished performers such as Ray Wilkins, Trevor Steven and Gary Stevens but it was essential to have a muscular presence too. Don't get me wrong. The so-called hardmen in our ranks could also play, and certainly in Hurlock's case he was a vastly underrated performer. But it did not do any harm for the opposition to know that they would be facing some of the toughest players around when the fixture was against Rangers.

The nature of the game in Scotland is that it is a hard, physical contest and you need people prepared to fight and scrap for the points. We knew we were regarded as the prize scalp and teams would be fired up when they were playing Rangers. There were some hostile places to go on wild winter nights and we needed strong characters capable of dealing with those occasions. Graham Roberts was in his element when the boots were flying and loved it when we became embroiled in a tough battle on a muddy pitch. For some players those conditions would be a turn off. Not Graham. The worse the circumstances the more he relished them. They were tailor-made for him and Rangers reaped the benefit.

I had played against him in England where he had rightly earned a reputation as a fearless competitor, and during his first season at Rangers he partnered me in midfield and the combination worked well as we won the title. The fans took to him in a big way, especially during one infamous clash with Celtic when he took over in goal after Chris Woods and Terry Butcher had both been sent off. He knew he was a big favourite with the supporters but in my opinion he seemed to think he was more important than some of his own team mates and that eventually led to an acrimonious departure back to England. In Butcher's absence he switched to centre-back and originally did a terrific job but it started to turn sour midway through the season after we had signed Richard Gough.

Graham and Richard were the new defensive partnership while Terry was recovering and there were signs that it was not gelling. It certainly did not work as smoothly as when

Terry and Graham were in tandem. In my opinion, Graham was becoming too big for his boots. He thought his popularity with the fans made him untouchable but it was more important to me that first and foremost we maintained a united dressing room. I was getting word that he was criticising some of the younger Scottish lads and making himself unpopular. Once I had been alerted to that I looked for the warning signs and it did not take me long to realise we had a problem. The team always comes first – ahead of any individual – and there was no way I was prepared to allow Graham Roberts to buck the trend.

As a player he did a great job but that became secondary when I realised he was becoming a disruptive influence on the squad. It all came to a head in a match against Aberdeen – again. I blamed him for their winning goal and bawled him out in the privacy of the dressing room. Some strong words were exchanged and his response was along the lines of 'if that is the way you feel about it you'd better sell me'. This was a direct challenge to my authority as manager and there was no way I was going to back down. I told him to 'consider it done'. He never played for Rangers again but I had no intention of giving him away cheaply. I held out for a realistic fee and it was some time before he moved on to Chelsea for £475,000, so we had made a profit on the deal for a player who made a big contribution for most of his stay at Rangers. It was good business but a sad end for somebody who had made a significant contribution to the cause.

I knew I had to win that battle because any suggestion that a player could undermine my position as manager would have had a knock-on effect right through the dressing room. He was a strong-minded character with an independent streak but I was not going to allow any individual to win a head-to-head with me. With the benefit of hindsight I am sure he wishes he had handled the situation differently. Only when he had gone did he realise what he had sacrificed because Chelsea were nothing like as big then as they are today. I had emphasised my position by standing firm and the message went out loud and clear: 'If you want to rock the boat at Rangers expect to pack your bags.' We had no room for malcontents and I would not tolerate anyone questioning my authority.

We have met since and there is no longer a problem between us. I don't bear grudges and I think he now accepts that when you challenge a manager's position there is only going to be one winner. He should know that now because he has managed clubs in England and I am sure he appreciates that he had placed me in an intolerable position.

We won the League Cup in 1988 but it was nowhere near enough for a club of Rangers' stature. I was not happy about that and was already planning to recapture the championship when we took our summer break. In many respects the next season was going to be the most momentous for both the club and myself.

On top of losing our title, it was made worse by the fact that Celtic had reclaimed it and, just to rub salt into the wound, they made it a double with the Scottish FA Cup. It turned out to be my most difficult season at Rangers and although we can all make excuses when it comes to injuries, we did really suffer in the 1987–88 season. Losing Terry Butcher so early in the campaign was a real body blow and we badly missed his inspirational quality. But the fact that it was Celtic who had finished ahead of us provided the biggest motivating force for the next season. It would have been bad enough if it had been Aberdeen or Dundee United but we could have coped with that. Celtic was the one team in Scotland our fans could not bear to see ruling the roost again and I knew we had to put that right the following season.

3

Player, Manager, Director, Shareholder

If life had been eventful in my first two seasons at Rangers, it paled into insignificance compared to the quite extraordinary developments which peppered the following year. We created a storm of controversy by signing a Catholic player and thereby finally breaking a taboo which had plagued the club throughout its history. In addition to being manager and registered as a player I became a part-owner of the club when David Murray took control. And – most importantly of all – we reclaimed the championship.

It was an incredible season for any number of reasons, yet when we reported back for training none of us had any inkling that the very fabric of the club was about to undergo a revolutionary change. Certainly all that was on my mind was winning the title but long before we had achieved that aim my position had radically altered and the club had been propelled into an exciting new phase.

When I accepted the job at Rangers my first priority was to restore them as Scotland's premier club. The ground had been transformed into the best equipped in Britain, the commercial side was booming, and I was beginning to stretch my own horizons. Europe had remained a back marker while we were concentrating on the domestic scene but the ultimate ambition was to make Rangers a force abroad as well as at home. I realised that would take time, and despite the disappointments of the previous season, so much was now in place. It was time for Rangers to make further progress. Nothing stands still in football and Rangers had the resources to become one of the giants of Europe. That was the target and although it did not happen during my time, or when Walter took over, I firmly believe that it is inevitable in these days of superclubs that Rangers will eventually take their place among the elite.

As each season goes by, football is edging towards a European Superleague and it is essential that Rangers are ready when that day comes. It will happen and there was further evidence of UEFA's plans with an expanded Champions League starting from the 1999–2000 season. It will take men with vision and ambition plus the courage of their own convictions to establish Rangers at that level and they already possess a leader in David Murray. I have mentioned elsewhere the contribution made by David Holmes when he was the chairman but after losing our title I sensed that perhaps he was growing a little weary of the constant pressure which comes with the job. The publicity machine never stops at Rangers and in 1987–88 not all of it had been complimentary.

I had known David Murray virtually from the first day I joined Rangers and have no hesitation in saying he is one of the most intelligent people I have met. He is a self-made millionaire, a man with the perception to see the bigger picture, and he has the limitless energy to make things happen. It was no more than a hunch at the start of the new season but I suspected that David Holmes and Lawrence

Marlborough might be ready to hand over the reigns. Eventually I was proved right but it took many months of meetings, discussions and negotiations and these were going on while the season was in full swing.

On the football side, Terry Butcher had made a full recovery from his injury and was ready to resume his partnership with Richard Gough. When I think of the key men I brought to the club over five years no other names were more important than these two. I had been chasing Gough for ages but it required the patience of Job and all my persuasive powers to eventually get him to put pen to paper.

I first met him when he was a youngster coming into the Scotland squad and you could see right away there was something different about this lad. He was so professional, even at that age. A natural athlete, he worked hard at his fitness, and it was clear he was going to be around for a long time. He was playing for Dundee United and I offered Jim McLean £500,000 to get him. The message back was he would not be sold to any Scottish club and he eventually moved to Spurs for £750,000.

I continued to watch his progress closely and although he loved the London life I was aware that his wife was pining for Scotland. Eventually we managed to convince Irving Scholar and David Pleat to accept a £1.5 million offer 12 months later. Cheap at the price in my opinion. To outsiders he seemed too good to be true. He was careful with his diet, totally dedicated to his profession, and he set an example to the kids coming through. People looked at him and thought he was a boring so-and-so because he geared everything towards his football and nothing was allowed to interfere with that. I knew what I was getting for that price.

Whenever we played five-a-side games nobody wanted to play against him. He had a wiry frame but he was all elbows and knees and he would knock you black and blue even in friendly workouts. He eventually took over the mantle from big Butcher. He had the same dedication and would always be one of the first to report for training and one of the last to leave. In the early days at Rangers the equipment for the gymnasium was sparse – and that is putting it mildly. The only people who went in there on a regular basis were Phil Boersma and myself. We have always been fitness fanatics and I wanted to improve the facilities to tempt more of the players to join us. Eventually we acquired a rowing machine and a bike and gradually the players would start to drift in for sessions after training. I call it a gym but it was so small it was really no more than a bootroom and we reached the stage where so many players were keen to join us we needed to set up a rota system because there was not the space for everyone to be in there together.

I knew we were on our way then because we had laid down the pattern and the players were following our example. The whole place was becoming more professional and it was characters like Richard Gough who influenced others to copy him. He fulfilled all my hopes for him and enjoyed a long career because he realised how important it was to take care of his body long before others came to the same conclusion. Today, fitness, diet and a sensible living style are essential but long before they became the norm Richard Gough knew they were key factors for any professional footballer. He was ahead of his time in that respect but we gained the benefit of the knock-on effect his example had on other members of the squad.

We were recruiting players left, right and centre in those days. Big names and lesser-known figures were arriving to bolster the squad. Ray Wilkins, Trevor Francis, Gary Stevens, Mark Walters, Kevin Drinkell, Mark Falco, Mel

Sterland, Andy Gray, Trevor Steven and eventually Maurice Johnston.

Some did not stay long but they all made their contribution and the main entrance at Ibrox resembled a revolving door as I wheeled and dealed, much to the resentment of other Scottish managers. They were moaning that I was pricing them out of the market and the game was on a rocky road towards disaster. Somehow I don't think players at other Scottish clubs were complaining because we were raising the stakes and they were getting the benefits in improved contracts. We had pointed Scottish football in a completely new direction and the reverberations continue to be felt today. My policy of signing English players to improve the standard has now extended well beyond the boundaries of the UK. Just look at the number of foreign players plying their trade in Scotland today – and not just at Rangers and Celtic. We were the pioneers but now everyone else has got in on the act. Whatever my critics may say they must now reluctantly agree this was the way forward because there are no boundaries in football any more. The insular, parochial attitude which prevailed in Scotland for so long has gone forever and not before time, in my opinion.

A chance remark from David Murray in 1988 led to me taking a stake in Rangers when he eventually took control of the club. He casually mentioned one day he would like to be kept informed if the club was ever likely to be put on the market and that set the wheels in motion for another big step in my football career. David's first love had been Rugby but he had toyed with the idea of buying his home town club, Ayr United, at one stage before he became involved with Rangers. Ayr turned him down!

Although there had been no official announcement from Lawrence Marlborough that he might be ready to sever his ties with the club, the thought was niggling away at the back of my mind right from the start of the 1988–89 season and I discussed the topic on a regular basis with David Murray. I wanted to plant the idea in his head that he was the right man to step in if there was to be a change of ownership and I could see the prospect appealed to him.

David was first and foremost a businessman and he realised there was enormous potential at Rangers. He could see what was possible because it was already beginning to happen and he knew it could be another money-spinning venture. I warned him if he became totally involved the danger was it would take over his life. He did not believe me at the time but if you ask him now I think he will agree that I was right. He is a man with the foresight and vision to plan ahead, yet he discovered, like so many others, that the world of football is totally different from any other industry. When you immerse yourself in this game everything else is forced to take second place. Your family life suffers and you become consumed by the demands and expectations, especially when you are the person pulling the strings.

We would dine regularly at Raffaelli's in Edinburgh and the subject would always be on the agenda. Months later I approached David Holmes and intimated that David Murray could be interested in buying Rangers if it became available. The response I received supported my theory that the owners were considering their position and I knew there was now a real chance it might just happen. I wanted to be fully involved and was prepared to put in a substantial amount of my own money.

David met with Lawrence Marlborough in October 1988 and a month later a price had been agreed for the change of ownership. It was in excess of £6 million. We were also inheriting an overdraft of several million pounds but we both knew the potential at the club and we did not regard it as a business risk. It took many more meetings before everything was finally agreed and there were a few hairy moments along the way – particularly when a certain Robert Maxwell appeared on the scene and threatened to hijack our plans. I was new to this side of football. The world of corporate meetings with lawyers and accountants was a new one for me and I needed to learn fast in order to keep up with the events which were unfolding. But it was all very exciting and when we finally put pen to paper I realised the full significance of what we had done.

Now I was a player, manager, director and shareholder! I was confident it would work well because David Murray and I were so close. Of course there was a shift in our relationship now. We were more than friends, we were business partners and although it has often been said it is a mistake to join forces with a personal friend in a business venture I had no qualms about that. We were both moving forward in the same direction and building Rangers into an even bigger force was all that mattered to us. When David Murray puts his mind to anything he devotes all his energy to the task, and that quickly became apparent when he took charge at Rangers.

I was in a unique position. I had a place on the board and I was the second biggest shareholder but I was also responsible for results on the pitch, and I did not forget that if they went wrong I could technically still get the sack as manager. That is always the risk for a manager and that would not change despite my newly elevated position. My first priority would always be the team while David concentrated on the business side of the enterprise.

David and I did make changes, and one was to appoint Alan Montgomery as Chief Executive. He came from a top position in Scottish Television with the task of increasing our revenue through sponsorship deals. David wanted to spend yet more money on Ibrox and it was essential that we explored every avenue when it came to fundraising. That was Alan's responsibility but I have to say we never really hit it off. Very quickly he had the biggest and plushest office in the ground and I knew we were on a collision course when he began to involve himself in the football side of the business. That was my territory and I had no intention of allowing anyone to interfere with what I was doing. And I was not the only one. It takes a lot to rile Walter but he came close to punching Alan in one incident when we were away at our Italian training camp in Tuscany – and you rarely see Walter lose his temper.

His row with Walter which so nearly came to blows summed up what the football people at the club thought about him. Walter is a quiet man, brought up with a typical Glaswegian philosophy on life. That is, 'I won't go looking for trouble but if it happens I will deal with it.' That night we were all sitting around the table having dinner and for some reason Alan was intent on winding Walter up all evening. He then involved David Murray's son who had had a couple of drinks and Alan thought it would be a good idea to take a picture of Murray junior surrounded by wine bottles. Walter immediately intervened and asked, 'What's your game?' Alan replied, 'What's it got to do with you?' and Walter went ballistic. He reached across the table for Alan and I have no doubt he was ready to punch his lights out before we were able to restore some order.

Don't let Walter's laid-back approach fool you. I gather when Everton was struggling against relegation towards the end of the 1998–99 season some of their fans were criticising him for not being more animated on the touchline when things were going wrong. Some people wear their emotions on their sleeve but Walter has never been that type. It does not mean he does not care. Quite the contrary. We all have different ways of doing this job and Walter was never a screamer and a ranter, and certainly not in public. But if any Evertonian ever doubted that Walter lacked passion they should have seen him that night in Italy.

Alan Montgomery did make some positive contributions – not least when we signed Trevor Steven from Everton. That was the first transfer to go before a transfer tribunal. Everton wanted £4.5 million for him but Alan led our delegation to the meeting in Lytham and spoke so eloquently we eventually landed Trevor for £1.7 million. He certainly earned his money that day but overall I had some terrible problems with him. I told David Murray one day he had a decision to make because I was finding it impossible to work with the man. I told the guy to his face, 'Let's get one thing straight. I don't like you and it will come to the stage where either you go or I go.' He went.

4

McCoist and Johnston

Contrary to popular opinion, throughout my time with Rangers Ally McCoist and I got on like a house on fire. Of all the characters I came across at Ibrox he is the one I will remember most for the laughter he brought as well as all the goals he scored. However, it is true I left him on the bench on many occasions and I also signed a variety of strikers which gave the impression I was always looking to replace him.

Colin West was my first signing. Other goalscorers who arrived included Kevin Drinkell, Mark Hateley, Andy Gray and Maurice Johnston but it was never my intention to send Ally packing and he knew that. He is a one-off and his presence in the dressing room was just as important as his contribution on the pitch. He was already well established when I arrived and I had my first glimpse of what was to come when we went on a pre-season tour to Germany at the start of my managerial career with Rangers. The first match was against Cologne and afterwards we attended a function in a wine bar. The place was overflowing with people and the joint was jumping. I had allowed the players to have a few beers when Ally came over to my table and asked if it would be OK if he sang a song.

I was expecting one of the Rangers anthems or a sentimental Scottish tune but instead he climbed on to a table and, using his beer bottle as an imitation microphone, let rip with a Bruce Springsteen classic! Suddenly the whole place went quiet and Ally had them eating out of his hand. He was up there for half an hour delivering a fantastic impromptu concert in front of an audience of amazed Germans. They loved every minute of it and so did I. Typical McCoist really: larger than life, game for a laugh and the only footballer I have ever come across who is loved by grandmothers, mothers, teenage girls and little tots. The whole female population seem to idolise him. He is blessed with a personality which makes him popular with everyone who comes into contact with him.

On the football side, I knew in Ally McCoist I had someone who was a natural finisher and a lucky player to go with it. I was also aware that I needed to keep on his case. He is the type of guy who is quick to take advantage if he thinks he can get away with it and I got the impression he was easing himself into the comfort zone so I decided to set a fire under him just to keep him on his toes. That is why I signed Maurice Johnston, another big-name striker who enjoyed the same popularity in Scotland. Ally christened himself 'The Judge' because he was spending so much time on the bench but I was regularly bringing him on and he continued to get his quota of goals.

Off the pitch Ally was still game for a laugh. The signing of Andy Gray produced a hilarious episode. I had played against Andy when he made his debut for Aston Villa against Middlesbrough. He was like Bryan Robson: his heart was too big for his body. They both went into tackles they had no right to go for because that was the way they played their football. They were fearless and they paid for it with a succession of injuries. Andy was living in the Midlands when I signed him and I agreed to allow him to continue training at West Bromwich and to join up with us on the Thursday or Friday before a game. So we only saw him occasionally and Ally decided he should have a full-time presence with the rest of the squad. One day he arrived with a full-size cardboard cut-out of Andy Gray – goodness knows where he got it from – and he placed it in the corner of the dressing room. Every morning, when the players reported for training, they would see Ally having a conversation with a cardboard replica of our latest recruit! Ally would say, 'Well, what were you up to last night, Andy?' and suchlike and this would go on for several minutes. That was him: the joker in the pack and there was never a dull moment when he was around.

I reduced him to tears on one occasion which showed the other side of his character. We had played poorly in a game at Ibrox and I came storming into the dressing room afterwards to let the players know what I thought of their performance. I turned to Ally and said, 'You are a dud.' 'No, I am not,' he said. I repeated, 'You are a dud' and this conversation went to and fro on the same theme until Ally burst into tears. Football being the game it is that was not the end of it. When we resumed training the following week Ally had a new name. When he had the ball all his team mates were quick to shout, 'Pass it to me, Dudley' and he was stuck with that tag for a few weeks.

That is the other side of McCoist. Deep down he is a sensitive lad behind the banter and the wisecracks. It does not surprise me that Ally has become a star performer on television. In fact he could carve out an even more successful career on the small screen after so many years at the top in football. He comes over as a natural on *A Question of Sport* and really it is just an extension of the way he conducts himself as a footballer. He is a lovely lad, a likeable rogue and is guaranteed to light up any room he enters. If for some reason I wanted to give him a roasting and summoned him to my office, I knew before he left he would have me doubled up with laughter because he would start telling me some story of what had happened to him the previous night, or if that did not work, a rendition of his latest joke, and I would be unable to contain myself. The word soon gets around if a player is on the carpet but I would love to have seen the expression on the face of any other squad member who made it his business to be near my office when he thought I was ready to wave the red card at Ally. What would they have made of the guffaws and belly laughs emanating from the other side of my door? Especially when they were all coming from me!

There was no nastiness in McCoist and he helped to promote the terrific dressing room atmosphere we had at the time. Sell Ally McCoist? Not on your life.

The Maurice Johnston transfer caused uproar in Scotland for obvious reasons. Rangers simply never signed Catholics. We were the Protestant club and Celtic had the monopoly on the Catholic boys. It never made sense to me but that was the way it had always been before I broke the mould and brought Johnston to Ibrox. I knew there would be fierce opposition in some quarters and that proved to be the case – and not just among the Rangers fans. There were divisions in the board-room and in the dressing room at the idea but the bottom line as far as I was concerned was if any player could improve my squad I would be interested in signing him. I had played with Maurice for Scotland and I rated him and that was all that mattered in my book.

At the end of the previous season I had come on as a substitute when we were beaten by Celtic in the Cup Final and I had thrown my loser's medal on to the dressing room floor. I was so angry I was talking out loud to myself and maybe the rest of the players heard me and suspected that I was determined to do something to make Celtic pay for that result. 'Those so-and-sos have got something coming, just you wait and see' was the gist of my ramblings.

Everyone assumed Maurice was joining Celtic when he was leaving France in the summer of 1989 and there was even a picture of him in the newspapers holding a green and white hooped jersey. I bumped into his agent after a game at Ibrox and just casually mentioned he might have told us Johnston was coming back to Scotland. He looked surprised and because of the Catholic situation suggested he had never even thought of contacting us. When I asked him what fee was involved and was told it was £1.6 million I told him we would definitely be interested. So began the groundbreaking transfer which was to end generations of tradition and put an end to a stupid policy which should have been scrapped years before.

I remembered the words of Jock Stein, a Protestant, who went on to become Celtic's most successful manager. He said if there were two star boys coming through in Glasgow, one a Catholic and the other a Protestant, he could afford to concentrate all his efforts on signing the Protestant because he knew Rangers would not be competing for the Catholic no matter how good he was. Celtic had overcome the sectarian barrier years before Rangers and had reaped the benefits. Kenny Dalglish is an obvious example. The fact that he was a Protestant did not deter Celtic from signing him. It was a one-sided argument and it was Rangers who were losing out for all the wrong reasons.

That was the way I saw it, so when Johnston's agent rang me back the day after we had talked at Ibrox to say Maurice was interested in meeting us I got straight on to the case. The first person I spoke to was Walter Smith and he was all in favour for the same reasons as me. Maurice was a class player and he could improve us. Next I raised it with David Murray and he was prepared to listen to my reasons for going all the way with this. His right-hand man, Jim McDonald, was initially dead against it – he thought fans would desert us in droves but I argued that a few goals from Maurice would win most people over. I accepted there would be some opposition but I was ready to deal with that. Eventually I was given the go-ahead to proceed with the transfer and flew out to France to meet Maurice and his representatives.

This had to be a cloak-and-dagger operation because if anyone had got wind of what was about to happen it could have collapsed at the first hurdle. I flew into Charles de Gaulle airport and Maurice's agent used Orly so there was no possibility of anyone seeing us together and guessing what was about to happen. In France we met at a little café outside Orly and thrashed out all the details over coffee.

When we brought Maurice to Ibrox to announce the signing, the rest of the squad had already departed for Tuscany and pre-season training. We had a press conference and then we both left for Edinburgh to take a private plane to Italy. We landed at a small airfield and completed the rest of the journey to the team's hotel by helicopter so we certainly arrived in style. It was a brave decision by Maurice to join us and he knew he would be under enormous pressure – especially in the early days. I had tried earlier to break down the barriers by signing John Collins from Hibernian. In the end it was the player who decided the implications were too great and he signed for Celtic instead. We provided Maurice with a bodyguard and he moved out of Glasgow to avoid any trouble. In that first season he was a model professional. He needed to win over the fans and even some of his own team mates. I remember some dyed-in-the-wool Rangers players in the squad would have nothing to do with him when he first arrived. Even the head of the Catholic Church in Scotland spoke out against the signing. The point everybody missed is that Celtic never recovered from our coup. We had snatched him from under their nose and they had to wait a heck of a long time before the championship flag flew over Parkhead again. They were badly damaged by that transfer and although I was not thinking about the implications for Celtic when he joined us, I cannot deny that I took a great deal of satisfaction that we had beaten our biggest rivals to one of the best Scottish strikers around at the time.

There was so much anger directed at him, and me, but he was the one in the spotlight because he was being judged by what he did on the pitch. And he did us proud in his first season. So many of his goals were the vital ones which won us matches or gained us a point. When we won matches by three or four goals he invariably scored the first one which was always the most important. The same applied in tight contests when you looked to him to snatch a goal and he duly obliged on several occasions. It took courage for a Catholic to sign for Rangers and I admire Maurice for taking the step despite the problems that he knew would come with it.

Now it is accepted that Rangers will sign Catholic players without anyone protesting and there are plenty of them at Ibrox these days but if we had not had the courage to sign Maurice who knows how long that ridiculous ban would have remained in place. He had a terrific first season and he steered clear of any trouble off the pitch. He was aware of the potential pitfalls and his behaviour was faultless. He stayed out of bars and deliberately kept a low profile but it all turned sour in the second year.

He was just not the same player. I sent him home in disgrace from our training camp in Italy and the story doing the rounds was that I had become involved in a fight with Maurice and that punches had been exchanged. That was the rumour when he arrived back in Glasgow and the press had pictures of the bruises on his face to strengthen their story. But it simply was not true. I was in my room and it was Phil Boersma who witnessed what happened. I gave the players permission to have a few beers one evening because they had been working hard preparing for the new season and there was a big row between Maurice and Mark Hateley. According to Phil it was all quite amicable until Maurice disappeared for a few minutes and when he returned he was a completely different animal. He had changed character and started throwing drinks around. Hateley got hold of him and told him to cool down, and the rest of the players needed to haul Mark off him. I could hear Maurice screaming and shouting from my room so I knew something had happened. My first inclination was to go downstairs and sort it out but again the wise words of Jock Stein stuck in my mind: 'Never look for confrontation as a manager because it will always come to you.'

The next morning Maurice claimed he could not remember what had happened and he didn't know how his face had become so marked. Again Phil got to the bottom of that. Maurice was rooming with Scott Nisbet who had removed Maurice's mattress from his bed and dumped it on the floor. When Maurice got back to his room he was feeling no pain and flopped on to his bed. Instead of a soft landing, his face came into direct contact with the springs supporting the bed. As Phil described it, it was like making contact with a buzz-saw although Maurice was not aware of it until he saw his face the following morning.

Maurice moved on to Everton after a second season with us but he was never the same again. Howard Kendall bought him for £1 million and then gave him a free transfer and he ended up in America. He did have a very good career in Scotland. He certainly lived it to the full. He played for Partick Thistle, Watford, Celtic and Nantes before I signed him. After his spell with Everton he joined Falkirk before eventually moving to America with Kansas City. He was terrific in his first season at Ibrox and overall averaged nearly a goal every other game in 100-plus appearances. You cannot ask for a better return for that from a striker and Maurice also revealed a strong sense of character by agreeing to join us when he knew it would antagonise so many Celtic fans.

He was the pioneer who ended a taboo which had plagued Rangers for generations. Now nobody questions a player's religion when he signs for the club and that is the way it should always be. I could never come to terms with that barrier. I am a Protestant but my first wife is a Catholic and two of my children have been brought up in the faith. How could I implement one rule as a football manager and then go home to a Catholic household and pretend to be someone else? It never made sense to me.

5

Manchester United and other Revelations

They say the best stories never get printed and I can just imagine what the reaction would have been if the two tales I relate here had become public knowledge at the time.

Would Manchester United fans have welcomed me as their new manager with all my Liverpool connections? Fantasy football? Oh no, the deal was virtually signed and sealed after an all-night meeting in Edinburgh.

In 1989 Michael Knighton had agreed to buy Martin Edwards's stake at Old Trafford for £10 million. It all seems very small beer today, especially when BSkyB valued the club at £623 million early in 1999. But in 1989 Michael Knighton was in pole position and a takeover looked imminent. There was just one small problem: he was finding it difficult to raise the cash after Martin Edwards had indicated he was ready to sell.

That is why he ended up in Scotland in a room full of lawyers, bankers, plus David Murray and myself. The meeting began at 9 p.m. and at midnight we stopped for a break and went to David's home where his wife got out of bed and cooked us a meal of bacon and eggs. Then the meeting resumed and by 3.30 a.m. a deal had been agreed and Michael Knighton was in a position to buy Manchester United. With everything in place we discussed future plans for the club. Remember, at the time Alex Ferguson was going through a difficult spell as manager and it was agreed that I would become the new manager at Old Trafford and Walter would take over at Rangers.

The deal eventually collapsed and Michael Knighton lost his great opportunity because David Murray had second thoughts the following morning. Questions were already being asked about Ken Bates, who had a stake in Partick Thistle and Chelsea, and David was reluctant to become involved in a similar controversy. Rangers had become his first priority and he was not going to jeopardise his interest in them although the prospect of having a say in a club the size of Manchester United had an obvious appeal.

Football was beginning to frown on anyone having a stake in more than one club. Robert Maxwell, with his Derby and Oxford connections, was also being investigated, and David did not want to become embroiled in a situation which might have caused embarrassment. Strangely enough, he was linked early in 1999 with Manchester City, although he remains firmly at the helm at Ibrox.

My other tale is of a bizarre experience I had with a famous Scottish international. UEFA were preparing to introduce a ridiculous rule which would limit the number of non-Scottish players to four the following season and that presented us with an obvious problem. We had many Englishmen on the staff, so it was a matter of urgency to add to our Scottish contingent.

I bumped into the player in question one night in an Indian restaurant in Edinburgh. He was playing for another Scottish club and I casually asked him if he would be interested in joining us the following season. It was not an illegal approach, more a case of two international colleagues having a chat over a meal and a glass of wine. He said he would like to come to Rangers but there was a small problem. He needed £30,000 in a hurry. He had a reputation as a gambler but I did not want to know what was going on in his private life. As this was a rather delicate situation I decided not to inform the chairman about the player's request and agreed to make him a personal loan without involving the club.

On the night I was due to meet the player with the cash, I dined with David Murray at Raffaelli's, and as we left the restaurant to get into his car a motorbike with a long, thin number plate on the back drove by. It was a highly unusual sight, with the sharp edges protruding on either side of the machine. It was not something you see every day and it stuck in my mind. The chairman dropped me off at my apartment and an hour later I left carrying £30,000 in banknotes for my rendezvous at Tynecastle which was only a matter of minutes away from where I lived.

As I drove away I noticed the same motorbike with the distinctive number plate at the end of my road. It was parked alongside a car and there was somebody sitting in the driver's seat. I was beginning to get suspicious and as I turned into the main road I was keeping an eye on my rear mirror. Sure enough the motorbike was behind me and 200 yards ahead was a set of traffic lights. I went through them on amber. I knew if he did not stop that I was being followed. He ignored the red light and stayed on my trail so I decided to take him on a bit of a wild-goose chase. Instead of heading for Tynecastle, I drove towards the area where I used to live. I know those streets like the back of my hand and I was on familiar territory. The bike stayed with me so I pulled into a garage to get petrol. The girl at the desk must have thought

I was crazy because I had filled it up earlier in the day and now I was stopping to put a pound's worth into the tank.

Out of the corner of my eye I saw the motorcyclist drive past so when I got back inside the car I called my brother Bill on my mobile phone and told him I had a problem and asked him to meet me at my apartment as soon as he could. I reckoned there was one of two scenarios unfolding here. Either the guy on the motorbike was checking that I was going to deliver the money or he was planning to take it off me. By now it must have been obvious to him that I was aware he was following me and when I reached my apartment my brother was waiting and the motorbike disappeared.

I did not want anything more to do with the player after that. To this day I have never asked him what it was all about but I would be curious to hear his side of it.

Other Scottish managers moaned about the money I spent at Rangers but I never paid more than £1.7 million for anyone. In England, transfer fees were considerably higher and if you look at the market today my deals were small beer by comparison. I was prepared to bring in what might be called nuts and bolts players to fill the gaps while I waited for the quality performers I wanted to build the team around.

Even when I left to join Liverpool the attacks continued. I remember Alex Smith, the manager of Aberdeen at the time and also chairman of the Scottish Coach's Association taking offence when I reminded everyone of something that was patently obvious – Rangers and Celtic were the dominant forces in the Scottish game. Surely nobody would challenge that query? Well, Alex did. He claimed that I had no credibility left in Scotland for making that remark! I wonder if he feels the same way today when he sees which two teams have taken a stranglehold on the Scottish championship. I accept that Aberdeen have had their moments but it is becoming increasingly difficult for any club to threaten the dominance of the big two in Glasgow. A similar situation is developing in England. Manchester United are way ahead of the rest with Arsenal and Chelsea attempting to keep up. But for teams like Liverpool, Leeds, Tottenham and Aston Villa there is a long road ahead before they can challenge United again.

For every Butcher, Gough and Gary Stevens there were others who played their part for only a fraction of the cost of my major buys. Yes, I was buying English players on a regular basis but I was always aware that there were limits and I could not spend just for the sake of it. Ray Wilkins cost just £250,000 in 1987 and that represents a bargain in anyone's book. I had played against him when he was at Manchester United and AC Milan but I believe he played the best football of his career when he joined us. He was one of those guys who improved as he grew older.

The crowd took to him instantly because they recognised he was a player with immense ability. He had played for England 84 times but when we went for him he was having a difficult time at Paris St-Germain. He had lost his place in the team so I thought we might have a chance to entice him to Scotland.

I flew to Paris to meet him in the week we were preparing to play Hearts, who were making a strong bid for the title. We managed to complete the transfer just in time for him to make his debut in that game. He had not been playing regularly in Paris but for 70 minutes he ran the midfield against Hearts before I took him off. Ray was a dream to work with. While we had more abrasive characters in the dressing room, Ray was a gentleman who put his own message across with the sheer quality of his performances on the pitch.

In his own way he exerted as similar a degree of influence as Butcher and Gough. And he could be a funny guy when the occasion warranted it. He had a dry sense of humour which rubbed off on the rest of the lads and it did not take long for the younger players to look up to him because he quickly commanded their respect. His honesty, integrity and sheer professionalism made him stand out. Any successful manager must have good characters in the dressing room and I appreciate how lucky I was to have people like Ray, Terry Butcher, Richard Gough and Mark Hateley, who also came into that category. They laid the foundations for what has followed at Rangers and I am sure the impact they had is still having repercussions to this day.

Being a top player does not guarantee you will become a good coach but if I was a betting man I would have placed every penny I possessed backing Ray to be an outstanding success in management. This has nothing to do with his record as a great player. I am talking about his knowledge of the game, his personality and the way in which he conducts himself. He has everything required to make it in a big way in that department of the game and it is a real surprise to me that it has not happened yet. There is still time and I would not rule it out because in my opinion Ray Wilkins is a class act.

I know a few people were surprised when I brought in Terry Hurlock from Millwall in 1990. He had a reputation as a hardnut but in my opinion he was a vastly underrated player. He looked a handful with his shoulder-length hair and muscular build but there was much more to him than that. He was a terrific kicker of the ball. He had some pace and everyone knew he could tackle. If somebody had got hold of him at an early age and pointed him in the right direction he could have played for England. His reputation went ahead of him. Because he had a poor disciplinary record he was never really given the credit for what he could do on the park. Rangers have always had aggressive players and Terry was certainly one of them.

There was a constant stream of arrivals when I was Rangers' manager. I told David Murray in my second season that it was important to give the fans a new face on a regular basis because that was the way the game was evolving. The public had this insatiable appetite for fresh names and as the leading club the demand was even greater at Ibrox. Football was edging closer to the world of showbusiness and you needed to whet the public's appetite by introducing famous names on a regular basis. I told David that foreign players rarely stayed longer than two years at any club. It was not a question of loyalty or a mercenary attitude; it was accepted as a fact of life. And it is beginning to happen in Britain now. I can see testimonial games becoming a thing of the past because very few players will serve ten years at any one club in the future. David appears to have taken what I was talking about on board because Rangers virtually brought in a brand new team at the start of the 1998–99 season and their reward was a clean sweep of the trophies in Scotland.

I bought people like Mark Falco, Kevin Drinkell, Mel Sterland and Nigel Spackman. All were proven pros who I knew were capable of doing a job for me even if it was in the short term. Drinkell, for example, scored an incredible 49 goals in 54 games – quite an achievement for somebody who cost £500,000 from Norwich. When we sold him to Coventry we made a healthy profit. Falco averaged a goal every two games in his short stay, while Spackman did so well there were moves to make him a naturalised Scot so he could play for the international team. Sterland was around for only a year but it was long enough to help us win the title with two goals against Hearts.

If Mo Johnston broke the sectarian divide, the signing of Mark Walters was just as significant. Rangers had not employed a black player for 50 years when I signed him from Aston Villa for £500,000 in 1989. He was recommended by Johnny Giles and his skill and ability to keep possession of the ball made a huge impact on the team. It was not easy for him at the start. The banana skins were flying on to the pitch and the verbal abuse was totally unacceptable, but Mark handled it all superbly. I subsequently took him to Liverpool when I went to England.

I defy any manager to claim 100 per cent success in the transfer market. Football does not work like that and I certainly had my own failures. I brought in a giant Dane named Jan Bartram but he could not handle the hurly-burly of the Scottish game. Strange really because he was built like Ron Yeats, the big defender who was the cornerstone of Bill Shankly's first winning team at Liverpool, and he was a karate expert too. His only problem was he did not like physical contact of any kind! A major handicap for any footballer.

The big money went on Gary Stevens, Trevor Steven and to a lesser extent Mark Hateley. Gary cost £1.25 million when we took him from Everton and he rewarded me with six outstanding years. A regular in the England team, he was a natural athlete and he missed only three games in his first four years.

Trevor Steven cost £1.7 million and was sold to Marseille for £5 million. He eventually returned to Ibrox when the French club was unable to maintain the staged payments for his transfer, so Rangers got the best of both worlds with Trevor.

In fact, after buying Trevor for Rangers I was responsible for selling him to Marseille even though I was the manager of Liverpool at the time! That happened when I had the bizarre experience of meeting the controversial Bernard Tapie for the first time. He was one of the most famous men in France, an entrepreneur who turned his attention to football and transformed Marseille into a major force before his fall from grace. He wanted to sign John Barnes from Liverpool and an initial meeting was arranged with some of his representatives in Manchester. Peter Robinson and I discussed the transfer with them but we could not agree a fee for Barnes and the Marseille people returned to France.

Two weeks later I received a call asking me to go to Paris to meet Tapie in an attempt to revive the deal. At the airport I was met by one of his staff – a giant of a man who could easily have doubled as a bodyguard – and I discovered just what an important man Tapie was in those days. Since then he fell from grace after the scandal surrounding the Marseille club but he clearly was a man of considerable importance when I met him. My 'escort' seated me in a fancy Alfa Romeo saloon and produced a blue flashing light from the glove compartment, placed it on the roof of the car and off we went. Traffic in Paris is notorious but everyone made way for us, presumably thinking we were on official business and racing to an incident. We went through red traffic lights, ignored speed restrictions and were even waved through potential traffic jams by uniformed gendarmes!

Eventually we arrived in one of the most fashionable districts in the city and drew up outside 20-foot-high wooden gates. When they opened, we drove into a courtyard and the staff of the house from the butler down were all lined up outside the house to greet me! It was quite a reception committee. When we went inside I met Mr Tapie for the first time and was led into a magnificent ballroom for lunch. It had a painted ceiling and the heavy French furniture which you associate with the aristocracy. A quite stunning house and I was being treated like a king. Over a memorable lunch he tried to re-open talks to sign Barnes but when I explained we were not prepared to drop our price he asked me to recommend somebody else and I suggested Trevor Steven.

After lunch, Mr Tapie left to catch his private jet which flew him to Sardinia where his private yacht was waiting and I went back to Liverpool on a commercial flight. I never did have a private yacht berthed in the Mersey!

Mark Hateley came from Monaco in the summer of 1990 and after a difficult start he won over the fans with his never-say-die attitude. I first met him at the Grand Prix in Monte Carlo but it was another year before I managed to sign him. Mark had proved himself in England and Italy before he went to France and I thought he would be ideal for us. You would never describe him as silky but he was a strong, courageous centre-forward, tailor-made for the Scottish scene because he refused to be intimidated by defenders and could look after himself. He was powerful in the air and if he got the ball on his left foot you always thought he might score. He was the ideal foil for McCoist and Johnston. A real man in every sense of the word. He would not stand for any nonsense on the pitch or off it.

When I look back on my years at Ibrox I had a terrific bunch of senior professionals. I thought the atmosphere at Liverpool was special when I was a player but I honestly believe it was even better at Rangers. We were bringing in players who had performed at some of the biggest clubs in Europe. And what an example they set to the others. They were the first ones to report in the morning, demonstrating their dedication and professional approach. And they were reluctant to stop training when the session ended. As soon as the bus dropped us off back at Ibrox they went straight into the gym. It made my job easier when impressionable young hopefuls saw how much work established players put in to maintaining their standards. It was a huge bonus for me. I knew we were creating something that would last and that the spade work had been done.

If I had any regrets about leaving it was not because I failed to enjoy the same success at Liverpool but in retrospect I left something behind at Rangers which was only just beginning. Europe began to occupy my mind only when I signed English players from abroad. I was still concentrating on establishing the club as the dominant force in Scotland but that was beginning to change with the influence exerted by players such as Wilkins and Hateley who had learned so much from playing for foreign clubs and were passing on their knowledge to the younger lads.

They were not all squeaky-clean characters but that helped to bond them together. On one occasion we were taking a golfing break at an exclusive location in Scotland and one of the lads smuggled a young lady into the hotel. They finished up in the snooker room and were oblivious to the camera which was filming their antics in detail. It was being recorded for posterity, much to the fascination of the security staff who were glued to the action in the privacy of their own room where all the monitors were housed. They were the only ones watching that night and if the newspapers had ever got hold of it all hell would have broken loose. Fortunately I was told what was going on and managed to persuade them to reluctantly hand over the evidence. I won't name the player involved and I am sure he will be grateful for that.

Looking at my managerial career to date I have to say that the first experience was the best. Nothing matched the Rangers years but who knows what might happen in the future? At Rangers I was still a young man and although with the benefit of hindsight I admit I made many mistakes, the support from the boardroom never wavered and I really appreciated their contribution only after I left. It was never the same at Liverpool: at the first sign of trouble, where I had normally had support from my chairman, I felt isolated.

Today chairmen have a much higher profile and people such as Ken Bates, Alan Sugar, Doug Ellis, Irving Scholar and Martin Edwards are as well known as the managers they employ and seem to revel in all the publicity they generate. Ron Noades at Brentford and John Reames at Lincoln took it a stage further in the 1998–99 season by taking sole charge of the football side of their clubs, while Michael Knighton did the same thing at Carlisle.

Even David Murray briefly flirted with a more hands-on approach after I left. He is a dear friend and a very clever man but I think he reached the stage where he thought he totally understood the game before he took a step back and realised that was not the case, particularly after some of the buys that were made after I had moved on. It takes an intelligent man to recognise that perhaps there is more than meets the eye to this game. You can have all the diplomas and degrees in the world, be a well-established businessman in your own field, but football is something else again. Your apprenticeship is conducted in the public eye, there are no second chances if you get it wrong, and there are thousands of fans out there who think they know more than you do. Football is in the public domain and if you drop a clanger there is no hiding place.

I am not making excuses for the way I behaved but I did have a lot on my plate. We were the biggest club in Britain – bigger than Manchester United at the time – and I was player-manager, a director and a shareholder. I was flying to Majorca every week to see my children and although I was not aware of it, I had a disease which was rapidly growing inside me. The pressure was relentless and perhaps it was a blessing that injury ended my playing career, otherwise who knows what might have happened. Having said that I still played one reserve game for Liverpool when I joined them! Why? Because I wanted to.

I tried everything to overcome the injury which eventually finished my playing career. Several key players were not available for the Scottish Cup Final with Celtic in 1989 and for ten days I pushed myself in training to make sure I would be fit for a place on the subs' bench. I worked with the rest of the players every morning and afternoon, and in the evening I would go to a disused Army barracks near my home and put in another hour of hard training. I came on for 20 minutes against Celtic and we lost the game 1–0. I knew I could perform only at three-quarter pace and as I was never the quickest in my prime, it was always going to be a struggle from then on.

I contacted Richard Smith, an expert in alternative medicine, who had helped to prolong Bryan Robson's career. He was considered the top man in his field. He worked for several Italian clubs and also had contracts with other clubs all over the world. We met in Holland and he sent one of his top men to Scotland to give me round-the-clock treatment. He lived with me for a fortnight and would lay me on the kitchen table and go to work on my calf with his elbows and fingers. Phil reckoned the guy was a masochist but I knew his job was to remove all the blood clots which form after a chronic injury. They harden like little ball bearings and with the friction he was applying the pain was excruciating. Others sessions took place at Ibrox. There was a steep flight of stairs in the old stand and I would carry him on my back up the stairs in an attempt to cure the problem. It helped to a certain extent but I realised I would never be fully fit again.

In Scotland I had bust-ups with players, I fell out with large sections of the media and although I believed I was right at the time I can accept now that I was also in the wrong on occasion. I was too hard on the players – both at Rangers and Liverpool – but I was still learning the ropes then and I know better now. Because we enjoyed immediate success at Rangers I thought my style of management was the right way and I was not willing to listen to the other side of the argument.

That is why Terry Butcher's glittering career at Rangers ended on a sour note. We are friends again now but when he left that was not the case. I had refused to co-operate with Scottish Television (STV) after I had been banned from the touchline for 12 months and I ordered all the players not to give any interviews to them. Terry ignored that, which left me with no option but to go public with my side of the story.

The Scottish FA had originally banned me for three months after an incident against Dundee United. We were winning the game but Dundee scored an equaliser in the 94th minute. Only the referee knows why he allowed the game to go on for that long because there had been no hold ups and no question of timewasting. The game ended in a draw and I had an argument with the referee afterwards. The newspapers carried a picture of me pointing to my watch as I asked for an explanation why so much extra time was permitted. That was when the Scottish FA stepped in with another ban but there was worse to follow. I was confined to the directors' box on match day and had to communicate by telephone with Walter who was down in the dugout.

In one particular game at Ibrox there was a problem with the phone, and I needed to get a message through to Walter.

Immediately above the players' tunnel STV had a gantry for their cameras. I came down from the stand and popped my head out of the tunnel to call Walter over. STV must have tipped one of the cameras off its tripod to get a shot of the top of my head. It is the only way they could have done it because I did not go down to the touchline and I was only in the tunnel for a matter of seconds. That picture appeared on television; the Scottish FA got hold of the tape and the ban was extended to 12 months. No wonder I fell out with STV.

Terry was being troubled by a long-standing knee injury but I was still selecting him on a regular basis. When I did leave him out of a game we had words about it, and when I saw him giving an interview to STV, I decided enough was enough. There is a dual carriageway outside Ibrox with an island in the middle where the lads parked their cars. From my office window I had a perfect view of Terry and STV's Jim White filming a piece for the station. My instructions had been quite clear. Nobody was to co-operate with STV and here was Terry going against my orders and I was witnessing it all from my office. A newspaper article from Terry was the last straw and I hit back. He had refused to play in a game against Celtic claiming he was injured and I went public with that.

Really, that was the beginning of the end of his time at Rangers and when the split came it was a sad event because nobody made a bigger contribution to the team during my time. He was the catalyst for everything that happened at Rangers. Richard Gough took over the mantle after he left but no Rangers fan will ever forget the impact Terry Butcher had on his club. He set the standards at the start and I don't believe there is anybody else who could have done the job he did in my early years at Ibrox.

Maybe I could have handled it differently, and I am sure

deep down Terry would agree that he was not blameless either. But at the time I was still a young fella and in many respects a novice manager. If a similar situation arose today I am confident I would have an alternative strategy, but you learn about these things only when they happen for the first time. Terry knows he earned a special place in the hearts of Rangers supporters. Not only did he perform magnificently for the team; he absorbed himself into the Scottish culture. He was not just a Sassenach earning a living north of the border. Once he arrived he became a Jock in everything but name and I cannot pay him a higher compliment than that.

Terry went to Coventry as player-manager in November 1990. He later managed Sunderland before returning to Scotland to open a hotel in Bridge of Allan. He is now a well-known broadcaster on Scottish football and is also involved with football in Dundee. In his time at Rangers he won three Championships and two League Cups but I never measured his contribution in silverware. He was a cornerstone of everything I achieved at Rangers and I cannot over emphasise the impression he made at the club.

6

Leaving Rangers

A baggage handler at Heathrow was the first person to tell
me Kenny had resigned as Liverpool manager. I was returning to Glasgow after visiting my children and the guy must
have recognised me because he called out, 'Have you heard
the news? Kenny has left Liverpool.'

It was a massive shock, even though you learn in football
that the unexpected is always liable to happen. I had left
Liverpool in 1984 after the European Cup win against Roma
but I had followed their fortunes from Italy when I was playing for Sampdoria and then from much nearer home when I
joined Rangers. Kenny was and always will be an institution
at Anfield. The star of the team I played in, he then went and
won a League and Cup double in his first season as player-
manager. It appeared everything was perfect for him at
Liverpool.

As I boarded the flight for Scotland that day it never even
crossed my mind that I might be his replacement. Mine was
one of the first names mentioned but that was understand-
able. Liverpool had been appointing people with links to
Anfield ever since Bill Shankly had stepped down. 'Promote
from within' was the creed of the chairman, the late Sir John

Smith, and it certainly seemed to work. After 'Shanks', Bob Paisley, Joe Fagan and Kenny continued the tradition and the trophies and medals kept coming.

Apart from myself, John Toshack and Alan Hansen were also being touted as possible contenders but I honestly never gave it a second thought at the time. I was already managing one of the biggest clubs in Britain. We were successful and I was allowed a free hand by chairman David Murray to do it my way. He was also a close personal friend and everything a manager could wish for. It was a high-profile job but he was always there to offer support.

Nothing in this world is perfect and I did feel at times as though I was living in a goldfish bowl because of the massive interest in Rangers. We were never out of the news, we were spending big money on international stars, we were the top team in the country – attracting all the attention – and as the manager I was constantly under the spotlight. If I say so myself, I was the most famous man in Scotland. There were some problems, however, on a personal and a professional level.

I had been banned from the touchline by the SFA and I had separated from my first wife. I was being followed along the motorway from Glasgow to Edinburgh on a regular basis by newspapermen looking for scandal. There were rumours about other women and it was all becoming something of a soap opera.

On the plus side I was living close to my family in Edinburgh, I was the second biggest shareholder at Ibrox and I knew I could stay for as long as I wished. I knew there was always a role for me at Rangers even if it was not as manager.

The image of football was changing drastically in Scotland. Ibrox was attracting a new breed of supporter. Executive boxes and corporate hospitality – it was all a far cry from the old days. The Hillsborough disaster too forced English clubs to build all-seater stadia and it was only then the game began to appeal to a wider audience. Instead of being the sport for father and son it became a family event, because the modern facilities were more acceptable to women and children. All this was in place at Rangers in 1989. They had experienced their own tragedy in 1971 when 66 fans lost their lives at an Old Firm game and that occasion marked the turning point for Scottish football.

A couple of weeks after Kenny left there was a call from a third party at Liverpool asking if I would be interested in the manager's job. I immediately answered 'thank you very much but no'. I thought that would be the end of it but the seed had been planted and it was only human nature to wonder privately what it would be like to go back. My spell at Anfield as a player had left me with nothing but happy memories of Merseyside. Those were my best years winning trophies and medals. It was the same off the pitch. Many of the lads lived in the Southport area to enjoy the fine golf courses. Others opted for the country life on the Wirral but I was a city boy and lived close to the club's Melwood training ground in the West Derby district. Two of my children were born in Liverpool and I felt totally at ease with the Scousers. They were warm, humorous and loved their football. Many of the people I knew during my time as a player were still at the club so perhaps it was only natural to daydream about what it might be like to go back.

Two significant events involving St Johnstone occurred just as Liverpool made contact for the second time. Both happened when Rangers played a game at Perth against St Johnstone. We had experienced a problem on a previous visit and you could say a member of that club's staff played a major role in my decision to leave Rangers. Everyone knows the Nora Batty character in the TV series *Last of the Summer Wine* but even she would run a mile if she ever met the real live woman I had the misfortune to deal with at McDiarmid Park. Her name was Agnes although most called her Aggie – I was calling her something entirely different by the time she had finished with me.

It is important at this stage to understand what was going through my mind. My first encounter with the she-devil of St Johnstone happened when one of my players was injured early in the game. It was Oleg Kuznetsov, a brilliant performer we had bought from Dynamo Kiev at the start of the 1989–90 season. He was the captain of the Russian team at the 1988 European Championships and it was a major coup to bring him to Glasgow. Rangers fans were drooling over his ability when he played against us in a pre-season friendly and some even claimed they had not seen anyone as good as him in the last 50 years. In his first appearance in a Rangers shirt he helped us to a 5–0 win against St Mirren but sadly his second game was against St Johnstone and he lasted precisely six minutes before suffering a serious knee injury which put him out of action for the rest of the season.

I knew he was in big trouble when he was stretchered off and I followed him into the dressing room. He was lying there in obvious pain and I asked Aggie to fetch him a cup of tea. She refused! The next time we went back my players cleaned their boots in the dressing room and we had brushed all the mud into neat piles and placed them in a corner to be collected. Not good enough for Aggie. She popped her head through the door and went ballistic. I asked her, 'What do you expect the players to do? We've just played a game of football and where else do you expect them to clean their boots?' She was in a foul mood and announced her intention to make a

complaint to the St Johnstone chairman, Geoff Brown. As she
stormed off up the stairs towards the boardroom I was right
behind her. She accused me of swearing at her and claimed it
was not the first time she had encountered problems with
me. Mr Brown said, 'I will look into it' and I replied, 'I am
here, look into it now.' It was all getting very heated before he
made the mistake of taking hold of my arm. I warned him of
the consequences unless he stepped back immediately and
this unsavoury scene was being witnessed by my own chairman David Murray. I cannot begin to imagine what was
going through his mind.

It was the final straw as far as I was concerned. The
Scottish FA had just increased my touchline ban and I began
to think I was becoming a marked man and people were
conspiring against me and the club. It suited the Scottish
media too, because any meaty story on Rangers sold newspapers. Rightly or wrongly I got the impression I was being
persecuted and the whole situation had become an uncon-
trollable monster.

A friend of mine, Ian Blyth, travelled back with me after
the St Johnstone game and on the way home to Edinburgh I
told him, 'I have had enough of this. I nearly became involved
in a fight with the St Johnstone chairman. This is becoming
unbearable. I have been offered the Liverpool job, what
would you do?' He replied, 'I would take it.' My mind was
made up although I had not made my feelings known
publicly and – more importantly – I had not discussed it with
David Murray.

Across the road from Ibrox is the Swallow Hotel which the
club used on a regular basis while construction work was
going on at the stadium. It was ideal for the players, with a
swimming pool and a sauna, and it also became a venue for
Walter, Phil and me. It was there I told them about my deci-

sion to join Liverpool. I said, 'We have been offered the Liverpool job.' I deliberately said 'we' because my intention was to take them with me.

They were very much in favour of it which was good from my point of view. Phil was excited at the prospect. It would be like going home for him. He had played for the club and was also a lifelong supporter. He could not imagine a more attractive prospect. Walter was also very keen which was important to me because I was prepared to turn the job down unless Phil and Walter were joining me.

Walter and I flew to London and met Liverpool chairman Noel White, and Peter Robinson at the Heathrow Holiday Inn. Walter expressed some concern about how his arrival would be interpreted by the existing backroom staff, Ronnie Moran and Roy Evans in particular. I could not see a problem with that because it was my intention to have Ronnie and Roy on board too. There was never any question of replacing them as they had spent their working lives at Anfield and knew the place inside out. I needed their expertise and input but also believed there was room in my future plans for Walter and Phil. These were two people I had worked with at Ibrox. I respected their loyalty and knowledge and felt confident they could integrate smoothly with the famous Liverpool bootroom staff.

Walter did have some misgivings on that score and after giving the matter considerable thought he decided against moving. He felt Ronnie and Roy might think their roles would be diminished if he came. I was very disappointed because Walter had been my right arm at Rangers and his advice and guidance had been invaluable to me, particularly in the early days when I was learning the ropes as a novice manager. Despite Walter's decision, my mind was made up at this stage and I knew I would be going to Liverpool. My next task was to do the best I could for Walter and I told him to stay in place at Rangers while there was a chance he could be appointed as my successor.

The decision to leave remained a secret at this stage but I knew I needed to have a look at the Liverpool team as soon as possible. The opportunity came when they played a match at Southampton. My wife and children were living in Guildford, just up the M3 from the Dell which I thought would provide me with a logical explanation if anyone started putting two and two together when they spotted me at the game. It was quite comical. Nudge, nudge, wink, wink time in the directors' box. A charade really as the Liverpool people were forced to put on their public face and express surprise at seeing me – the manager of Rangers – attending one of their games at the other end of the country. I took my father with me and at half time I told him I was going back to Liverpool. He was all for it because he understood the problems I was having in Scotland but I knew it would be a wrench to leave him behind in Edinburgh. I had left home at the age of 15 to join Spurs and it had been a long and winding road back via Middlesbrough, Liverpool and Genoa, and now here I was packing my bags again.

It was going to be difficult to inform David Murray that this was the best way forward for me. I don't suppose there are many managers who socialise five or six times a week with their chairman. That was our routine and I believe we had a unique working relationship. In the beginning I admired the man for his business acumen but by the time I was preparing to leave we had developed a strong personal bond and I was not looking forward to informing him of my decision.

We both lived in Edinburgh and David rarely came to Glasgow, except for games and board meetings. He gave me a free hand to run the club and I often wondered how many other managers enjoyed such a privileged position. Every morning on my way to Ibrox I would telephone him from my car, contact him again after training had finished to keep him up to date with events and by late afternoon I would be back in Edinburgh in his office as we laid our plans for the next stage of Rangers' development. He liked to eat early and most evenings we would be in our favourite Italian restaurant by 7 p.m. David is a clever and perceptive man and he probably knows me better than anyone else so he sensed there was something on my mind the night I was preparing to tell him I was resigning. He never mentioned anything in the restaurant and drove me home to my apartment. As we arrived he turned to me and said, 'You're going to Liverpool, aren't you?' And that was when I told him.

It was a mild March evening and we sat on the wall outside my home. We talked for at least half an hour as he tried to persuade me to stay while I attempted to explain how the Rangers job had become unbearable for me because of the non-stop pressure and publicity. He fought hard. He asked me to go to his office the next day when he would draw up a new, improved contract. He said, 'You stipulate how long you want it to be for and how much you want paying and I shall sign it.' From a financial point of view the easy option was to stay but this was not about money. I wanted to lead as normal a life as possible and that was becoming increasingly difficult in Scotland. As a player I had become well known but the profile I now had was entirely different. For the first time in my life I was discovering what it really felt like to be famous and I did not enjoy all the baggage that came with that. I thought it would be different in England with the opportunity of a more relaxed style of living. I reasoned there were 50 million people south of the border as opposed to only

5 million in Scotland and it would be easier for me to melt into the background.

When David realised he could not change my mind I recommended Walter to take over, but David favoured a big-name replacement. I argued it would be in Rangers' best interests to appoint a lower-profile figure. The hard work had been done and a solid foundation was in place. After years without any success they were now the top club in Scotland again and I knew Walter was a highly respected figure in the dressing room. He knew how the place worked and had played an instrumental role in reviving the club. In the end David gave him the job and it did not take Walter very long to justify his appointment.

As for me, some prophetic words from David would come back to haunt me over the years. 'You will regret going back to Liverpool,' he said. Whatever gave him that idea?

It was a huge decision to leave Rangers. I had won three championships and they were well on course for number four when I announced I was joining Liverpool. In addition we won four League Cups but the one that got away was the FA Cup. It seems I am fated never to collect that medal. It never happened for me as a player for Liverpool and when we did win the trophy when I was manager I gave my medal to one of the players who was not included in the 16-man squad. In fact the only time I played in a winning cup team was in Italy for Sampdoria.

7

Back at Liverpool

Peter Robinson, now the Liverpool Executive Vice-Chairman, spelled out the size of the task facing me once I had agreed to take over from Kenny Dalglish. I knew Peter well from my days as a player and captain at the club and was confident I could work with him. His contribution to Liverpool's success goes right back to the 1960s when he arrived as secretary. In those days Bill Shankly was the boss and the two of them struck up an instant rapport. Shanks was the man rightly credited with transforming Liverpool from a run-of-the-mill Second Division club but behind the scenes Peter Robinson was also playing his part.

Over the years he has become acknowledged as the game's outstanding administrator and I am sure he would have become a senior figure at the FA if he had wished to go down that road. Instead Liverpool became his labour of love and his fellow directors have every reason to be grateful he decided to devote all of his working life to Liverpool. I have been told there was only one occasion in his 30-odd years at Anfield when he was tempted to leave and that was when Bill Shankly was offered the manager's job at Sunderland and he wanted Peter to go with him. In the end Shanks stayed put and so did Peter but that episode merely under-lined how close the two men had become.

Peter became recognised as the kingmaker at Anfield. He was the influential figure who convinced a reluctant Bob Paisley he could succeed Shanks and I know he was also heavily involved in the appointments of Joe Fagan and Kenny Dalglish. When I was given the job I took it as read that I enjoyed his support and I knew I would not have a problem in the boardroom while Peter was in my corner. Any manager needs to know he has the backing of the key men at his club – that was why I wanted to bring Walter Smith and Phil Boersma to help me on the training and coaching side. In the boardroom I knew I had an important ally and when he talked frankly about the problems facing the club I listened intently because Peter Robinson knows more about Liverpool FC than any other man.

His fear was always that Manchester United might get it right one day and if that happened they could take off in a big way and leave everyone else behind. When I played at Liverpool any success United had seemed to be magnified in the press. It suited the coaching staff at Liverpool to promote that idea. They argued most of the press were pro-United because they had grown up supporting the club. I don't know if that is true but we were taught to believe they were the city slickers and our best way to counter them was to win all the major trophies. Now the roles are reversed. United have come good and are the undisputed top team in the country. They have done it with a combination of the work ethic, some inspired signings and the best crop of home-produced players anywhere in the Premiership. By contrast, Liverpool were labelled 'spice boys' after I had left, meaning a highly paid team which has the potential to be successful but constantly underachieves. Now United have regained pole position it

Outside my home in Genoa, Italy with Trevor Francis before taking
my first management job with Rangers.

With John Paton, who was chairman at Rangers when I first joined the club.

With friend and colleague, Rangers' chairman David Murray.

Directing operations on the pitch as player–manager.

Bringing Trevor Francis to Ibrox. David Holmes is on my right.

The English invasion. Getting the signature of my captain at Rangers, Terry Butcher.

Chris Woods and Graham
Roberts celebrate winning
Rangers' first Premier
League championship under
my management, in the
1986/7 season. (*Above*)

Terry Butcher holds up the
Premier League trophy at the
end of the 1988/9 season. (*Left*)

With my assistant at Rangers, Walter Smith.

Maurice Johnston in action. The first Catholic player to sign to Rangers.

©ALLSPORT

Rangers' first black player, Mark Walters, causing problems on the wing against Aberdeen's Stuart McKimmie.

©ALLSPORT

A great goalscorer and a terrific player to have in the dressing room: Ally McCoist.

will be very difficult to dislodge them and it won't necessarily be Liverpool who manage it if and when United lose their way.

In many ways Peter was accurately predicting the future for both United and Liverpool when he discussed the task ahead for me. Despite all the turbulence which marked my time as manager, my opinion of Peter Robinson never altered. I trusted him implicitly and established a similar relationship to the one I enjoyed with David Murray at Rangers. I considered myself fortunate to have such an experienced ally because in a football environment, when the pressure is really on, some managers discover to their cost that not everything is as it appears on the surface. I never had such misgivings when I was dealing with Peter Robinson.

As soon as I walked through the door the first thing he said to me was, 'You do know what you are taking on, don't you? We are not a good team and we don't have many great players. In fact we only have one – John Barnes.' Unfortunately even that did not turn out to be the case. It did not take me long to realise that Barnes's best days were behind him and that was a major blow because I was hoping to build my team around him. At one stage of his career he was the best player in Britain. Sadly, that was before I came back as manager, and his failure to produce what I required was one of the many disappointments I endured as manager.

Peter warned me, 'this is a big, big job' and that opinion was echoed by another director, Tom Saunders. Tom was the liaison man – he would be at Melwood every day to observe what happened on the training field – and wear his director's suit in the boardroom. A former headmaster, he had been recruited by Bill Shankly after managing the English Schools team. He knew his football and so when he said, 'Do you like a challenge? Because you certainly have got one here' it was a gentle reminder that he did not expect it to be all plain sailing. Over the next two and a half years there were many occasions when Tom would sidle up to me and whisper, 'I told you it would be a challenge and now you know.'

When the story finally broke in the newspapers that I was leaving Rangers there was no turning back. I had always promised myself that if I ever left it would be through the front door of Ibrox. Any manager knows the sack goes with his job and although I was secure at the time I was never so naive as to think it might not happen to me one day. I was proud of my achievements at Rangers and if it had all gone pearshaped I vowed I would leave with my head held high and not scuttle away through the back door. Unfortunately that is what happened but there was a valid reason.

As I've already shown, the signing of Maurice Johnston by Rangers in 1989 created an uproar in Glasgow. He was the first Catholic to join the club and some of our fans were outraged. I knew I would be criticised in some quarters and predictably the press had a field-day. After the transfer had been announced I suggested Maurice and I plus some of the club officials should make a public appearance in front of the fans waiting outside the ground.

We walked down the marble staircase and when I opened the front door there were a few hundred supporters present. Some of them were burning their season tickets and others were setting fire to their blue and white scarves. When I turned around to see who else had come to the door with me there was nobody there! Don't ask me where they had all gone – my friends and colleagues must have found something else to do. All I knew was I was facing an angry crowd on my own. It remains to this day a mysterious moment. So when I resigned as Rangers manager they made sure I departed through a side door, presumably because they did not want a repeat of the scenes which marked Johnston's arrival. A club official had obviously tipped off the directors that a crowd was gathering to witness my departure. I was sorry to leave under those circumstances. Whatever people may think about me I am an up-front type of person and the only thing I was guilty of was making the decision to join Liverpool.

Phil Boersma was in the car with me when we drove away from Glasgow for the last time en route to another press conference in Liverpool to announce my appointment as manager. I remember stopping at a motorway service station to break the journey. It was at Killington Lake in Cumbria. In my own mind there were no doubts about the move. I had spoken to my father and my two brothers and they all understood why I was going back to Liverpool. More than anyone they realised what I had been going through at Rangers and they believed I had made the right decision. I looked across the water at Killington and thought to myself, 'Well, this is it – let's get on with it.'

I drove into the car park on that April day at Anfield to see many familiar faces waiting for me. That felt good – a sign of the stability which has been one of the great strengths of Liverpool over the years. Not just the players and backroom staff, but other people who have spent their working lives there in a variety of roles. It is reassuring to know there is continuity – it tells you that the place is being run efficiently by people who have only the best interests of the club at heart.

I could not wait to get started. I was so excited at the prospect although I had not forgotten the words of warning from Peter and Tom, and through the grapevine I discovered that Kenny had been prepared to come back and take the job.

When he resigned he took a break in America but I was told he was making arrangements to discuss a return when he learned that I had been appointed. As I saw it I was coming home. Just looking at the pictures and paintings of previous successes adorning the walls at Anfield was a reminder of the great days I had enjoyed as a Liverpool player. My best years had been spent wearing the famous red shirt and this was where I had learned to become a professional footballer. When I moved from Middlesbrough in January 1978 I was a bit of a Jack the lad, a would-be playboy to be honest about it. I was young, single and enjoying the good life. At that age you think you know it all and when a top club like Liverpool wants you perhaps it is only human nature to think you have got it made.

It did not take me long to realise how little I did know, just by observing the way senior players conducted themselves at Liverpool. With all due respect to Bob Paisley, Joe Fagan and Ronnie Moran, my real soccer education came from players such as Ray Clemence, Steve Heighway and Phil Neal. They taught me how to become a good pro on and off the pitch. Yes you could go out and enjoy yourself at the appropriate time and most of the Liverpool lads liked a drink – there was no secret about that – but I needed to be reminded there was a time and a place for everything. It was not a holiday camp they were running at Anfield and if we occasionally let our hair down socially we certainly put in the work on the training ground, and those players pointed me in the right direction. I was taught to train well every day and when it came to Saturday you were ready for anything. That was the Liverpool way as I remembered it and it worked.

The good habits were passed down from one generation to the next and I like to think that when I left, others coming through had learned by observing how I behaved. It was the same with Kenny Dalglish. A young player only had to watch how Kenny conducted himself. If you could produce a photofit depicting all the best attributes required to be a top-class footballer you would end up with Kenny, the consummate professional.

When I returned I looked around the dressing room and saw several senior pros and I thought the old ways would continue to apply and these footballers would be the role models for the next batch coming through. In my opinion it was their job to educate, encourage and occasionally bully the younger players and lead by example. To my thinking, the success of the club should be more important than anyone's bank account. Within a few months of being back at Anfield it seemed to me that there were no leaders in the dressing room any more. Instead there were plenty of individuals concerned with the value of their next contract. Then there were the testimonials. As a player I spent seven years at Liverpool and during that time only Emlyn Hughes had a testimonial. While I was manager Nicol, Whelan, Rush, and Grobbelaar had testimonials and Jan Molby and John Barnes were waiting their turn.

It seemed to me that the passion for the club had disappeared and that was a massive shock for me. I could not believe it when senior players would say they were looking for one more big move. Why would they even contemplate leaving Liverpool? This was the place every player used to dream of joining: number one in Europe – never mind England – and the change saddened and angered me. The team spirit had gone and that was another blow. You cannot expect a diverse squad of players always to hit it off but the 1980s team always stood up for each other. Even on a night out if a problem developed for anyone he knew the rest of the lads would back him to the hilt. That was the bonding spirit which also showed itself on the pitch. Now it appeared to be a thing of the past and was reflected by the team's performances. I needed no reminding at that point of the words of Peter and Tom – and this was only just the beginning.

8

The Problems Begin

It took less than two months for me to realise the Liverpool of 1991 was a pale shadow of the club I had left in 1984. I found the change of mood in the dressing room both startling and alarming. How could standards have slipped so badly? Where was the pride in wearing the shirt? We felt ten feet tall before a game when we came down the tunnel beneath that famous sign which proclaimed: 'This is Anfield.' Time was when that sent a quiver of apprehension through any visiting team. Nobody liked playing against us in our own backyard and the roar of the crowd as the players emerged on to the pitch made it one of the most intimidating arenas in the country. It was the fixture nobody fancied, Liverpool away – the one to avoid. Our reputation was such that some teams took heart from an honourable defeat. Few expected anything more, but times had changed.

I remember before one game when I was manager, a visiting player – I was told it was Vinnie Jones, then of Wimbledon – had scrawled 'Bothered' across that sign. It was a sarcastic response to a symbol which meant so much to the team I played in. If it had happened during my days as a player it would have been like a red rag to a bull but my team just made a joke of it. They thought it was funny. By laughing it off instead of being wound up, they were copping out – typical of them. There were a few individuals in the 1980s team who would have gone looking for Vinnie, despite his reputation as a hardman. Not now though.

I remember another indication to me that the Liverpool of 1991 was not able to cut the mustard. Peter Robinson asked me if I wanted to take charge of negotiating players' contracts and I said yes. He was paying me a compliment by giving me that responsibility but it turned out to be a mistake because it placed me in an awkward position with some of the players. This was the time when salaries were beginning to escalate rapidly and I found myself with players grumbling about the wages the new signings were being paid, while others had their own agenda and were looking to move on and make a financial killing of their own. The world of professional football is a small one and you hear most of the talk on the grapevine.

I knew Peter Reid was keen to take Steve McMahon to Manchester City and I knew Everton was interested in Peter Beardsley, so it was no surprise to me when both players came into my office and hinted they were ready to move on unless there was a guarantee of regular first-team football and improved terms to go with it. They were suggesting they had the opportunity to join other clubs and because they were around the 30 years of age mark it was an attractive proposition to get a big new contract elsewhere. I could not get my head around that because Liverpool had always been the place to be. I did not want to leave but I had no choice. My first wife needed to be out of the UK for tax reasons and that is why I joined Sampdoria. Why would I want to quit Liverpool as a player? I had just captained them to a European Cup success and I was captain of my country. I remember one day on the way to training David Johnson turned to me on the team bus and said he had heard a rumour I was being sold to Manchester City. That night I had a nightmare and woke up in a cold sweat because I believed Liverpool had let me go. That is how much it meant to me to play for Liverpool. I was so relieved when I realised it was not true. I don't know if there was any substance in the story but I did know Liverpool was the only team I wanted to play for. I could not imagine a better place to be, so my reaction to any dissidents was to get them out of the door as soon as possible. That was the wrong approach. What I should have done was keep them for another year and buy myself some time to bring in replacements, but the idea that a top-class player wanted to leave Liverpool was simply beyond my comprehension, and I unwittingly played into their hands by letting them go too soon.

These were experienced players, well capable of doing a job for me but I was impetuous and recommended we sell if the price was right. It was a major error. I was the first Liverpool manager since Bill Shankly to be deprived of the luxury of buying players and giving them time to acclimatise in the reserves before being thrust into the limelight. Guys like Ray Kennedy and Terry McDermott had served their time in the reserves before becoming established – that was the way it worked at Liverpool. My signings had to go straight into the team and I did not help myself by allowing other senior play-ers to leave before the replacements had been bedded in.

When Kenny reads this he won't be surprised because I told him the same thing to his face during the 1998–99 season when we were both in London to host an FA Cup draw. He knew there was major surgery required to his team – the biggest since Bill Shankly changed everything after a cup defeat at Watford back in the late 1960s. Part of

Liverpool's success after that was they never allowed a similar scenario to happen again. If they thought any player was showing signs of coming to the end they would sign a potential replacement a year in advance and give him the time to learn the Liverpool way. That had been the format beginning when Shankly broke up that famous team of the 1960s. But I felt Kenny allowed that policy to slip and I can understand why.

After the Hillsborough disaster, Kenny and his players went through a horrendous time. After all the emotion of that traumatic time, coupled with the stress and the many funerals they attended, Kenny could not say goodbye to those players. And those were the players I inherited. Even the fans must have known that half the team was past its sell-by date and there was nobody waiting in the wings to take over. It was too early for Steve McManaman, Robbie Fowler and Jamie Redknapp, who were rated as promising youngsters for the future. Kenny had become very close to his players as people rather than footballers and you cannot blame him for that. But it made my job so much more difficult. I was the first manager since Shankly with a team which was not going forward. Bob Paisley reaped the benefits of Shankly's work, built on it and passed it over to Joe Fagan. The team Kenny was handed had reached the last two finals of the European Cup but I was the first to inherit a team going backwards. At the time that did not register with me. I had such a high opinion of myself after achieving success at Rangers I thought, 'Hey, this job is easy.' If I could have looked at the situation with the benefit of hindsight I would never have moved to Liverpool when I did. But I convinced myself that despite the obvious weaknesses I could prevail – that was how confident I felt about my own ability.

There were other headaches at this time. The two big

summer signings in my first year were Mark Wright and
Dean Saunders and the newspapers were speculating about
how much money we were paying them. I remember Ray
Houghton and Ian Rush, among others, knocking on my
door demanding explanations. 'We have won this and we
have done that for this club so why are these guys earning
more money?' was the general question. I tried to explain
that salaries were beginning to rocket and these players
were fortunate to have made big money moves at the right
time for them. But that was no consolation to those earning
less – they were hardly paupers by the way – and I was put
in a situation where I was refusing them parity and then
demanding they go out and give me 100 per cent in the next
game. That caused some bad feeling and it was the beginning of a downward spiral in my relations with some of the
players. Eventually I fell out with most of the guys who
were at Anfield when I returned. One of the reasons was
that I could not accept the lack of determination and fire in
their bellies to win games for Liverpool. I had remembered
it as a unique place. Whether it will ever be the same again
is difficult to say.

When I was a player we were winning championships and
European Cups but the hunger for more was always there.
Ronnie Moran was constantly reminding us that we were
never as good as the old teams when Ian St John and Roger
Hunt were the stars and after them came the era of Kevin
Keegan and John Toshack. That would motivate us and we
would try to make him eat his words. And it was always the
club which benefited. I wanted to recapture those days but I
was banging my head against a brick wall.

I became tired of certain players telling me the game had
changed. Some claimed it was much quicker and more aggressive but that did not cut any ice with me. More aggressive? I

thought the hardmen were being phased out. My players told me it was no longer possible to play the way the old Liverpool teams did. The bottom line was they were no longer good enough to win the major trophies. Six years earlier as young players they could do it because in those days they had a few guys on the pitch who could lead them by the nose. There were no leaders when I went back. Any manager who has a couple of characters to inspire the team is a lucky fellow and he has got half a chance of being successful because the rest of the team will follow people like that. If they see somebody prepared to stand up and take anything that comes their way you will find the rest will quickly follow suit and stand shoulder to shoulder with them. I did not have that type of person in my team. Sure we could still play some pretty football and dominate teams at Anfield if the circumstances were right, but on a less than perfect pitch or when there was a wind blowing and a hostile crowd on our backs we simply could not deal with it. Previous Liverpool teams were capable of digging out results but the team I had could not. They could perform when they were on top and all look like good footballers but in the past Liverpool had been renowned for being able to deal with any situation. It used to be a case of 'Do you want to play football against us or do you want to fight us? It does not make any difference because either way we can cope.'

The team I was responsible for would throw in the towel if everything was not going their way. The lack of support I received from the dressing room was one of the reasons why I was not a success as Liverpool's manager. If you don't have the players on your side you cannot win because they hold all the power in the modern game.

I first saw evidence of this attitude when I was at Sampdoria. If a star player was unhappy with the coach he would go to the club president and complain and if the results were not going well the president would listen and the coach could be on his way. Such behaviour was unheard of in England in those days but as the game has become more popular and so many players have become millionaires, they have started to wield considerable power well beyond the dressing room. If you have a star player coveted by other clubs it is now vital that you keep him happy and if the manager or coach needs to be sacrificed to make that happen then so be it.

The Bosman Ruling has also brought a significant change. There has never been a better time to be a top professional footballer. Not only can you earn money beyond most people's wildest dreams but you can also pick up a massive signing-on fee at the end of your contract – either from your own club which is desperate to keep you or by leaving on a free transfer and taking a big percentage of the transfer fee your new employers no longer need to pay. Phil Boersma and I often discuss how the great managers of yesterday would have coped in the present climate and you have to say they would have found it stunningly difficult. People like Bob Paisley, for example. He was never the type to get involved with agents and the growing band of hangers-on who inhabit every big club today. And the endless wrangling for money would have left him cold. I have to say I don't think Bob would have been able to handle it on his own, and I am talking about the most successful manager in the history of the British game: that is how much it has changed.

Bear in mind, when I returned to Liverpool it had been roses all the way in my career, apart from one temporary setback at Tottenham. After playing for Scotland at schools and youth level I was signed by Spurs and went to London convinced I was going to be a superstar. I was young and headstrong but supremely confident in my own ability and in next to no time I was hammering on the manager's door demanding to know why I was not in the first team. Not exactly the ideal attitude from an unknown and it came as a real shock to the system when Spurs said they were prepared to sell me at the age of 19. That pulled me up short and I went to Middlesbrough determined to prove Spurs wrong and show them what they were missing. I never looked back after that: the move to Liverpool, a couple of years in Italy and then the plum job as player-manager of Rangers. I had 54 Scotland caps, all the trophies and medals, and by anyone's standards I had enjoyed a terrific career. I did not want that record spoiled at Liverpool, but there was much worse to come, both on and off the pitch.

9

Alas Smith and Thompson

When I joined Liverpool as a player, Tommy Smith and Phil Thompson were well-established stars in the team and I thought I got on famously with the pair of them. They were always in the thick of the battle – local boys who had achieved their goal by reaching the top and representing the club they loved – and you could see that every time they pulled on the red jersey. Now I like to think I played with passion and I recognised kindred spirits in these two. Football was all about winning in my book and Tommy and Phil had the same attitude. Different types of course. Tommy was an intimidating figure who had built up a reputation as a defender to be feared and his name always featured when forwards discussed the guys they wanted to avoid. Usually the top three would be Norman Hunter, Ron Harris and Tommy – in no particular order. Phil was tall and skinny but with a burning ambition to be a success, and he was one. Apart from all he won at Liverpool there were 42 England caps just to emphasise that he had made it at international level too.

Socially we were also friends and I regularly went out for a pint with Phil and Terry McDermott. It was Tommy who introduced me to the person who was to become my father-in-law when I married for the first time. That was at the old Holiday Inn in Liverpool when we all attended a dinner after Chris Lawler's testimonial game. Phil also went out of his way to help me settle on Merseyside when I first arrived. He would be on the telephone inviting me for a night out and showed me around the city. It was a different story when I returned as manager and Phil and Tommy became among my biggest critics. It certainly changed my perception of them as people and I found it difficult to comprehend how individuals can display such a change of character. Were these the same two guys I had enjoyed spending time with when we were players? Perhaps they resented me coming back as the boss and taking a role they wanted for themselves. Tommy had worked at the club for a short spell after his playing career ended and the word was he had the choice of staying on but decided against it. Phil was the reserve team coach when I returned so he already had one foot on the ladder if Liverpool were to continue with their policy of appointing ex-players to responsible positions.

Everything seemed to be the same way when I came back. Tommy was on the after-dinner circuit by now and writing for the local newspaper. Phil had a DIY business, apart from his job at Anfield, and it never crossed my mind I might have a problem with him even though a few years earlier Bob Paisley had taken the captaincy from him and given it to me. That was not an issue as far as I was concerned. I am not the type of person to bear grudges, and I was quite content to let Phil get on with his job while I concentrated on mine.

Reports began to filter down from the boardroom that the directors were unhappy with some of his language at reserve games. Remember hardly a soul goes to watch these matches and when Phil started shouting and bawling, his voice would echo around a near-deserted ground. Usually the only other people present would be friends or family of the youngsters playing, a couple of directors and scouts from other clubs. Now, industrial language goes with football – I have been guilty of using it on many occasions – but when there are 40-odd thousand fans shouting their heads off, the words emanating from the dugout are easily drowned out. It is a different situation at a reserve match and Phil's cursing and swearing could be heard by everyone within earshot. I was not unduly concerned and knew he was passionate about his job but his antics were causing some concern in the boardroom. I was asked to have a word with him about it and I told him to tone down the comments. It was not a reprimand because I did not think that was necessary, but there were more problems to come.

Steve Heighway was in charge of the kids at Anfield and I was getting word that some of the youngsters he was recommending for promotion to the reserve team did not want to take the step up because they knew all about the verbal abuse Phil would dish out to his team. Steve is one of the best youth coaches in the game and played an important role in the development of young stars such as Robbie Fowler and Michael Owen. He is a highly respected figure at Anfield and enjoyed the trust of parents and kids alike. It was very important for the club to have a figure who commanded such respect and it gave Liverpool a big advantage when it came to attracting outstanding prospects to join the club. On one occasion, my secretary begged me to intervene when a furious row between Steve and Phil threatened to get out of hand. Her office at Anfield was next to Steve's and she could hear them going at it hammer and tongs. The language was embarrassing and she feared they were about to come to blows. The row was over how Phil was treating some of the lads who had come through the ranks under Steve. They had gone back to complain to him and Steve was letting Phil know exactly what he thought of him.

Because of my mistaken loyalty to Phil I never made a major issue of what was going on and was prepared to allow him to continue with his job providing he modified his language and toned down his behaviour. The big bust-up with Phil was entirely his fault but I would not expect him to admit it because it's not in his character. I was in a Manchester hospital recovering from my heart operation and Ronnie Moran had taken charge of the team as caretaker boss, with Roy Evans as his right-hand man. The season was coming to a close and our FA Cup Final against Sunderland was just a couple of weeks away when Manchester United came to Anfield needing a win if they were to pip Leeds for the old First Division Championship. Leeds played on the Saturday morning and beat Sheffield United and Liverpool beat United in the afternoon so the title went to Elland Road. In my enforced absence Phil had upset Ronnie and Roy by suddenly promoting himself to fill the gap I had left and to make matters worse he was trying to dominate the team talks before games.

After the United match he went into the bootroom and started criticising everything I had done as manager. Now that would have been unacceptable in any circumstances but when you have the visiting manager and his coach in attendance it becomes unforgivable. United were our biggest rivals and although we maintained friendly relations with Alex Ferguson and Brian Kidd, you simply don't go badmouthing your own people in front of guests. It shows a divide in what should be a united club. Alex was not present when the comments were made but he told me he is aware of what happened because he was informed by Brian Kidd. Alex and Brian are not the types to start spreading the word around the game that something was seriously wrong at Liverpool, but such an outburst was embarrassing and damaged the image of the club. I am told Roy tried to intervene and stop the tirade but Phil just ignored him. He blamed me for everything. He slammed my policy in the transfer market, he ridiculed my buys and blasted me for allowing certain players to leave. He accused me of trying to change the training programme – anything he could think of he laid at my door. In his opinion I was wrong to have switched the day-to-day routine away from Anfield to the training complex at Melwood.

You may wonder how I knew all about this when I was in a hospital bed 35 miles away. The answer is Brian Kidd was so shocked by this attack he rang Archie Knox the same evening. Archie had been United's assistant boss before returning to Scotland to work with Walter Smith at Rangers and he and Brian had become close during their time together at Old Trafford. Brian told Archie what had happened and Archie passed it on to Walter. That is why the next day he found it necessary to drive all the way down from Scotland to inform me what was going on at my own club. I remember him saying, 'This is not the best time to be telling you this after such a major operation but you need to know a member of your staff has been criticising you behind your back. I am sorry it has to be me to give you the details but we are mates and I feel it is my duty to tell you'.

I will always wonder why Phil delivered such a critical attack at this time. Was he jumping on the bandwagon because of the article I had written in the *Sun*? Or was it a simmering resentment going back to when I took the captaincy off him? Whatever the reason his actions were inexcusable and I decided he had to go.

At this time Tommy Smith was also condemning me in the

local newspaper and on the after-dinner circuit. I was not the most popular man on Merseyside but if I could not do anything about how the public perceived me I could certainly take action when it involved somebody who was supposed to be working with me. I told Peter Robinson I wanted Phil out of the club. The matter went before the directors and there was not one objection. Instead of shaking heads I saw nodding heads all around the boardroom table. Nobody spoke up on his behalf, nobody tried to intervene, nobody objected – there was not a single dissenting voice. I was back on my feet – after a fashion – when we won the cup and I was determined to tell him face to face that he was out of the door because I believe that is the right way to handle these issues. The decision had been taken and now the season was over it was the right time for a parting of the ways. But Phil pre-empted my plan because he was in such a hurry to collect his Cup Final bonus. All the backroom staff were due to receive one and he went to Peter Robinson's office to ask for his. Peter told him he needed to speak to me first because I had something to tell him. I remember I was in my car when the phone went and it was Phil demanding to know what was on my mind. This was a Friday and I told him I would see him in my office the following Monday. But he wanted to know there and then so I told him, 'I'm sacking you.'

Phil sued the club for unfair dismissal and eventually accepted an out-of-court settlement. He was out of the game for six years but he wrote a newspaper column and barely a week went by without some barbed comment about me. I'm not surprised it took him six years to get back in. And if I was the only one with that opinion, why didn't Roy Evans re-appoint him when he took over from me? I can honestly say I never anticipated having a problem with Phil when I was the manager but perhaps that proves we can all be naive at times. You never stop learning in life, do you? Now I have had time to reflect on a couple of minor spats we had had over the years and wonder if they had contributed to this sad state of affairs. The first came in Dublin. We were over there to play a friendly game and we all gathered for a drink in the Burlington Hotel. I had just got married to my first wife and for no reason in particular – he was probably trying to be smart – Phil accused me of getting married because my wife came from a wealthy family. I tossed my pint of lager over him and threw a punch. We were separated by the rest of the lads and nothing more came of it. The second was when he became captain of the team and it wasn't working out. It came to a head when we lost to Manchester City on Boxing Day and dropped to 12th in the League. That was to mark the end of his reign as skipper but the writing had been on the wall a few weeks earlier. Bob Paisley had asked him if the responsibility of being captain was proving too much for him and for his pains he received an unprintable reply. Bob may have looked the paternal type but he could be a hardman and he never forgot those who crossed him. Phil effectively lost the job when he gave Bob a mouthful in front of the rest of the lads.

When Bob offered the job to me it came right out of the blue. I was standing behind the goal on the training ground while the rest of the lads were having some shooting prac-tice. I was not involved because I had turned my ankle, so I was watching when Bob sidled up to me and said, 'Do you want to be captain?' I said I would love it but there were a few people in front of me such as Phil Neal and Kenny Dalglish and I did not want to upset anyone. He said that was his problem and he would deal with it. Forty-eight hours later I had been appointed Liverpool captain. My first game with the armband was a victory at Swansea in the FA

Cup and despite our lowly League position at Christmas we went on to win the Championship that season. I was captain for three years and very proud to have been given the opportunity. Phil may have thought I had gone behind his back but he was wrong. That was the story put about when Emlyn Hughes succeeded Tommy Smith and it was an open secret that those two never got on after that but it was never my style to go and ask for somebody else's job. Phil had dug his own grave by then. It is true I always enjoyed a solid relationship with Bob Paisley. He sometimes had trouble explaining himself because he was not the most articulate person but I never had a problem understanding his Geordie dialect. I had lived in the North-East when I played for Middlesbrough and I found it quite easy to relate to his thoughts and actions.

At that time, we had fallen into a daily routine because we lived quite close to each other. Bob had a friend in West Derby who owned a garage and on the way in to training he liked to call in there for a cup of tea and to check the racing pages before placing a couple of bets. I was up and around at the same time taking my children to school and I got into the habit of joining him every morning. We had time for a five-minute chat at the garage and I soon understood his terminology and what he was talking about. But I was never seeking to gain an advantage over the other lads. Yes, I hit it off with Bob, but I was not the only one.

When Roy Evans left and Phil was appointed assistant manager to Gerard Houllier I found it hard to believe the club had taken such a decision. But time changes everything and we're talking football here, so anything is possible. It has nothing to do with me what they decide at Liverpool but I had to smile when I saw Phil's comment after his appointment. 'I always loved Liverpool more than I hated Souness.'

At least he finally admitted what he thought of me. Good luck to Gerard Houllier. I hope he enjoys the experience of working with Phil more that I did.

At the end of the day I feel really sorry for Tommy Smith. In my eyes he is sad figure these days and far removed from the fearsome character who wore the number four shirt with such distinction for Liverpool. In his pomp as a player he was an inspirational defender epitomising the passion and fire Bill Shankly demanded from his players. He was a powerfully built competitor who combined physical strength with an ability to pass the ball accurately over any distance. And he could wind up faint-hearted forwards just by talking to them out on the pitch. They call it sledging in cricket but Tommy had mastered the art long before that word became fashionable. He was never backward at coming forward, and threatening all sorts of retribution to opponents was part of his gameplan. Perhaps I should have taken more notice of that side of his character when we were team mates because when he decided to make me his enemy he let his mouth run away with him.

In my opinion he is nothing less than a hypocrite. I shall remember him not as the 'Anfield Iron' but as a little man trading on his past glories. It has taken me a long time to get around to replying to some of his comments over the years but now is the time to set the record straight. The battle lines were clearly drawn when I banned him from the Anfield bootroom. There was nothing personal in that. I would have taken the same action against anyone else in the circumstances and I know I was absolutely justified in making that decision. The ban I imposed remains in place to this very day – he is still not allowed access.

When I came back to Liverpool, Tommy had his regular column in the *Liverpool Echo* and a postbag in the *Football*

Pink in which he added his comments to readers' letters. His articles were becoming increasingly critical yet all the time he seemed to be under the impression that he had the freedom to go where he liked at Anfield simply because he was an ex-player.

After a match he would be in the bootroom sipping a lager and chatting away with Ronnie Moran, Roy Evans and the visiting manager and coach. My players could see him as they walked down the corridor to their own lounge and were entitled to think I was condoning what Tommy was writing because he was allowed to socialise with the staff. It was wrong and I knew I had to put a stop to it. He was now working for the press and they had their own facilities provided by the club. I failed to see why Tommy should be an exception when all the other journalists accepted certain areas were off-limits.

I rang him before one night match to explain as politely as I could why he was no longer welcome in the inner sanctum and I suspect I made an enemy for life after that call. I told him he had put me and the coaching staff in a difficult position and he had to understand that he was now on the other side of the fence. He could not expect to enjoy our hospitality when he was going into print criticising the players and the club. The players were entitled to think I had no problem with his articles when he was still allowed to roam around the place without any restrictions.

I tried to explain why I had taken this course of action but after that our relationship went rapidly downhill. He took every opportunity to put the boot in and some of his attempts were quite pathetic. For example, he made an issue of the fact that I lived in Cheshire and commuted to Anfield, implying I should be living on Merseyside. That was nonsense and so petty. It took me 35 minutes to drive in – it took some of the

Southport-based players longer than that – but he was looking for anything, no matter how trivial, to have a go at me.

When I sold that story to the *Sun* he must have thought he
had won the lottery. Now here was something he could really
get his teeth into. I make no attempt to defend myself for
entering into that arrangement with the *Sun* but I certainly
don't have to defend myself to Tommy Smith. There are no
excuses for what I did and I shall try to explain the circumstances later. The rights and wrongs of it had nothing to do
with Tommy Smith but he became like a dog with a bone and
would never let the matter drop. So let us be clear about
Tommy Smith and the *Sun*. He has written many more articles for that newspaper than I ever did – and he was paid for
them. Liverpool fans knew it too because the evidence was
there in back copies of the newspaper. But Tommy denied
ever working for the *Sun* and even had the gall to go live on
Radio Merseyside with his denials. To make matters worse
he continued to put his name to articles in the *Sun, after* the
Hillsborough tragedy, despite repeatedly denying he did so.
Now there are lies and damn lies but this one was a beauty.
Perhaps the old memory is going Tommy. So just to remind
you what you really did here are a couple of examples. One
headlined: 'Thank God I don't play now – I just could not bear
to kick a ball again.' Check your bank account, Tommy – you
were paid £500 for that one and it was all about the
Hillsborough disaster. You were still at it nearly two years
later with another paid piece about Kenny's resignation.
'Even Shankly quit under pressure' was the headline. Have
you forgotten that one too?

He wrote many pieces for the *Sun* over a number of years
but he used the *Echo* to churn out all his invective against
me. I was portrayed as the villain of the piece with Tommy
appointing himself as my judge and executioner. And it did

not end there. On the dinner circuit he was telling sick jokes at my expense to try and raise a cheap laugh. One of his favourite lines was the suggestion that what a pity it was that I did not do everyone a favour and die on the operating table; that the doctor should have turned off the life-support machine. I'll let you be the judge of these comments.

10

The Transfer Bazaar

There is one facet of soccer management which is always closely scrutinised by supporters and that is your policy in the transfer market. There is no hiding place in this aspect of your work. You buy and sell players, and the fans debate the rights and wrongs of your judgement. Naturally their opinions will be coloured by results and they will be quick to jump on your back if you have replaced one of their favourites with a new man who fails to deliver.

If you believe everything you hear about me in the transfer market I was an unmitigated disaster and I stand accused of bringing a once great club to its knees. The harsh truth is Liverpool were in decline when I arrived and you can trace the origins of their fall all the way back to Heysel. Yes Kenny Dalglish did the League and Cup double the following season – a magnificent achievement in his first year in charge – but it was the last throw of the dice by the last great Liverpool team which had reached European Cup Finals in the previous two years. You could argue that to have reached the pinnacle again in those circumstances was an incredible feat and I would agree. But Heysel, tragically followed by Hillsborough four years later, took its toll on the club.

My brief as Liverpool manager was to introduce new blood as quickly as possible into an ageing team. Yes, I was guilty of trying to change too much too soon but at Rangers I had supervised a massive turnover of players and we had been successful. You have to believe you are right when you buy but we all make mistakes too! I cannot think of a single manager in the game – from Alex Ferguson down – who can honestly say every one of their purchases was a success.

I am the first to admit some of my buys for Liverpool did not come up to scratch. I was also guilty in some instances of being influenced by the advice of people at the club who persuaded me to sign players I was not totally convinced would meet the standards required. Again I take the responsibility because the bottom line is I had the final say and I cannot deny that. I mentioned in a previous chapter that I off-loaded some players too quickly and paid the consequences but in other cases I felt justified in allowing certain individuals to leave because they were simply not good enough. Jimmy Carter, David Speedie and Glen Hysen came into that category. Steve McMahon, Peter Beardsley and Ray Houghton had their own priorities at the time because they were approaching the veteran stage and were looking for another move. With hindsight I should have kept them at least another year while I shopped for replacements but I was not prepared to wait because there was a massive rebuilding job to be done.

Of all the players who left Anfield in my time the only one I wished I had kept was Steve Staunton. He was a young Irish lad with a sweet left foot and was capable of playing in a variety of positions. It was just unfortunate that a ridiculous new rule was introduced while I was in charge which classified non-English players as foreigners and decreed you could play only three of them at any one time. It was nonsense. For the first time in my life I was technically an immigrant in my own country! When you looked at the Liverpool squad it was clear the implications could be potentially disastrous for us. We were not exactly overrun with Englishmen.

Liverpool has always been a cosmopolitan team. The FA Cup-winning side of 1986 did not include a single Englishman. When I took charge there were players from Zimbabwe, Denmark, Sweden and Israel plus the Irish, Welsh and Scots. There was an urgent need to recruit more English players to plug the gaps. That was the only reason I sold Staunton, and Ron Atkinson was first in the queue, taking him to Aston Villa. The irony of it all was that the regulation was withdrawn a year later and Staunton is now back at Anfield. But while it was in force it created havoc and had a direct bearing on how we assembled our squad.

I gave my growing army of critics plenty of ammunition when expensive buys struggled to become established – but they conveniently forgot the new faces who did arrive to provide excellent service for the club. I am not attempting to dodge the issue because it hurt me as much as any fan when a player fell short of expectations. In a sense it was their money I was spending and we all wanted the same thing – a winning Liverpool team. I saw John Barnes as the main man but I also knew Jan Molby had the passing skills to be a key figure. On separate occasions I took them out to dinner in Knutsford to outline my plans for the future. Jan always had a weight problem and I emphasised the need for him to keep in good physical shape if he was to be a force in the team. Jan is an easy-going guy but I was always looking for more from him because his talent had never been in doubt. It never quite worked out that way because bad habits are hard to break and Jan enjoyed his lifestyle off the pitch and consequently his game suffered. As for John Barnes, I failed to get through to him. That was a big disappointment because at one stage of his career he was a class act – but those days had gone by the time I became manager.

Whenever the subject of my buying is discussed, the names of Paul Stewart and Nigel Clough usually top the list, simply because they cost big money and never made an impact. OK, that is fair enough and I will explain later why I invested so heavily in them, but there were others who certainly gave value for money. I spotted Rob Jones playing at Crewe and paid £500,000 to bring him to Anfield. He was only a young lad but he had pace and I took a gamble by putting him straight into the side against Manchester United and told him to mark Ryan Giggs! That is what you call going in at the deep end but he did a terrific job and he was playing for England in his first year at Liverpool. He has been particularly unfortunate with injuries otherwise I am positive he would have gained considerably more than his eight caps. Anyone suggesting he was a bad buy? I don't think so.

You can add the names of Mark Wright, Michael Thomas, Neil Ruddock and Dean Saunders to the list even though none of them, for a variety of reasons, were able to deliver everything I wanted. Wright, in my opinion, was the best central defender in the country when I signed him from Derby. He is a complex character and we did have our rows during his first year, basically because I had so much faith in him and he occasionally thought I was demanding too much. He did not think that when he held the FA Cup aloft at Wembley following the victory against Sunderland in 1992. Mark was one of those guys who felt he needed to be 100 per cent fit to perform at his best, but there are some occasions when players must put the club first and play through the pain. Admittedly he did suffer from a series of injuries that constantly interrupted his career but he went on to play until he was 34 before a back problem forced him into retirement. When I left Liverpool he took the trouble to telephone me and admit he had eventually realised the message I was trying to get across to him and I appreciated that.

Mark's big pal at Derby was Dean Saunders and I recruited him to play alongside Ian Rush. They were partners in the Welsh team and knew each other well so I was confident they would forge a potent combination. Dean is a bright, lively character who played football with a smile on his face – and he was a proven goalscorer. He hit 23 in his first season at Liverpool but I sold him the following year and lived to regret it. Rushie had come in to see me and said the partnership was not working. Other people at the club felt he was not good enough and I allowed myself to be influenced by their opinion. Since then I have signed him twice, taking him to Galatasaray and Benfica and he has continued to score goals.

Michael Thomas scored a title-winning goal for Arsenal at Anfield and was the type of midfield player we needed. Again injuries hampered him but he was an honest, hard-working player and he never let me down when he was fit. I took him to Benfica when Liverpool released him.

It seems Liverpool have been searching for a strong central defender ever since I left but when I signed Neil Ruddock to play alongside Mark Wright I was confident I had the combination which would serve the club well over a long period of time. 'Razor' was big and not afraid to use his strength. He had the physique to frighten forwards, an accurate left foot and he was strong in the air. He was a bouncy character, always game for a laugh, but perhaps that was his undoing. When I signed him he was exactly what I was looking for but when he looks back on his career I suspect he will realise he did not fulfil his potential. Not everything in his life was right. He had a problem controlling his weight – maybe he liked a night out too much – and there were other factors which contributed to him not achieving as much as he should have. A pity, but he won't be the first or the last footballer to think if he could do it all over again he would handle some aspects of his career in a different manner.

Julian Dicks could be difficult to handle, but when match day came around you knew what you would get from him. In his earlier days he got saddled with a reputation when his naturally aggressive style earned him a 'wild young man' tag but he never let me down. If there was a young Julian Dicks out there today I would not hesitate to sign him. I never had a real problem with him but Ronnie Moran did. Julian was set in his ways when he came to Liverpool and did not take kindly to Ronnie's training methods. That caused some friction between them and after I had left and Roy Evans had taken charge I am sure Julian knew the writing was on the wall and he was living on borrowed time. Sure enough, he was one of the first to go after I had left. In my opinion he was as good as Stuart Pearce. He was unfortunate to play at the same time because that cost him the opportunity of playing for England. There was very little to choose between them. Julian had a bad disciplinary record which counted against him with the people at the FA but he was the type I would have liked in my team when I was a player because he never ducked a challenge and he was always first in the queue when the going got tough. He went back to West Ham where he is rightly regarded as some kind of folk hero.

David James is not everyone's favourite goalkeeper but I believe he has been unfairly blamed for some of Liverpool's defensive frailties over the last few years. I can remember when Bruce Grobbelaar was the first choice and he made some horrendous errors. And David did not have the benefit of playing behind men of the calibre of Phil Neal, Alan Hansen and Mark Lawrenson. I cannot help wondering how Bruce would have coped with the defenders who were supposed to be protecting James. Yes, he makes mistakes – show me a keeper who doesn't – but it seems he is always the fall guy when it goes wrong for Liverpool. I would rate James on a par with Grobbelaar but time can play tricks with people's memories. Most Liverpool fans will recall Bruce with affection because he was an extrovert and a great shot-stopper. I would argue that James is equally adept in that department but there is no hiding place for a goalkeeper. When the team is struggling he is always the first to be singled out.

I admit there were others at Anfield who were not totally convinced by James and we did make a move for Tim Flowers before he joined Blackburn. To be frank I did not think he was any better than James but we did propose an exchange deal which would have taken James and Mark Walters to Southampton and Flowers to Liverpool. In the end he decided to join Blackburn but I was not too disappointed when he turned us down.

Mark Walters had his moments at Liverpool but was never fully accepted by the fans. He had a hard act to follow because he was the replacement for John Barnes who was out for most of a season with an Achilles injury. Comparisons were constantly being made between the two and it was inevitable that Mark would suffer when the Liverpool fans remembered the golden years of Barnes. As I have mentioned above, the Barnes I worked with was no longer the powerful winger with the scoring touch. The acceleration had gone and without that he could no longer unlock defences. When he did start playing again he preferred a less arduous role as a central midfield playmaker. He always retained his ability on the ball; he could hold it up, rarely lost possession and passed it accurately but the Liverpool fans remembered the vintage Barnes, and Mark Walters would never claim to have been in that class. He was a better player than he was given credit for and did a terrific job for me at Rangers. He was already established at Aston Villa when I first bought him but if he lacked anything it was a touch of steel. He was the type who needed encouraging because his confidence could be easily dented and he could have done without the comparisons with Barnes.

I bought Paul Stewart to provide the muscle in midfield. I had kept tabs on him for a number of years and Walter and I were interested in taking him to Rangers when he was a centre-forward at Manchester City. We watched him on a number of occasions but I was never quite sure of him as a striker. He was strong and willing and made things happen but lacked some sharpness in and around the penalty box. On one of our visits to Maine Road we did not bother to book our tickets in advance and paid at the gate. It was mid-winter and I was wearing a scarf around my face to keep out the cold. Peter Swales, then the City chairman, learned we had been at the game and made some sarcastic remark about our secret spying mission being a failure because he knew we were in the ground. That was not the case. I prefer to be well wrapped up in winter; it was as simple as that.

Eventually Paul moved to Spurs and they converted him into a midfield player. I remember George Graham, who was at Arsenal at the time, writing an article in which he said Stewart should be in the England team. He earned a Man of the Match rating when Spurs won the FA Cup in 1991 and somebody else must have taken note of George's comments

118

because Stewart did get his England call-up. We made some enquiries and it soon became evident that Paul was very keen to join Liverpool. He was a Manchester lad with his family based in Blackpool and he wanted to move back to the north-west. Unfortunately it did not work out for him at Liverpool. Goodness knows he had the desire to succeed but sometimes moves do fail and this one certainly did. It is difficult to pinpoint any one reason why and I know it certainly was not for lack of effort. He was desperate to establish himself at Liverpool but the bottom line is he did not and we had to recognise he was not going to be the man for the task.

Nigel Clough was another one who did not make it although on the surface he had everything going for him. He was an England international and enjoyed an excellent career with Nottingham Forest. He was an intelligent lad who had been well schooled in the game by his famous father. He was also a bit of an introvert, but the general consensus at Liverpool was that he would fit in easily because he had the passing skills and vision to complement our style. He was lined up to be Ian Rush's new partner but Rushie was soon complaining again that this was another combination that was not going to work.

I have to admit Nigel was not my first choice when we signed him. I had been tracking David Batty at Leeds for a long time and was on friendly terms with Bill Fotherby, a Leeds director who eventually became chairman. He assured me we could get Batty at the end of the season and I was giving my board regular updates on the situation. They felt we should sign Nigel because his contract was due to expire and we were sure to get him, and they were reluctant to wait for Batty just in case he decided to stay at Leeds. They were different types of player and once again I was primarily in the market for that elusive figure to play the physical role in midfield after it became clear that Paul Stewart was not the answer.

There were other failures on a smaller scale. I paid £250,000 for Istvan Kozma, a Hungarian international. He was at Dunfermline and I remembered how he had always caused Rangers problems when we played them. I classed him as a low-risk buy because the amount of money involved was modest, but he never came to terms with the pace of the English game and I was forced to concede that he was another investment that failed.

Torben Piechnik is another name that crops up when the anti-Souness brigade are in session. Tom Saunders and I went to watch him play for Denmark against West Germany. He was marking Karlheinz Riedle, who later moved to Liverpool, and he kept him quiet all night. On the basis of that game we decided he was worth keeping an eye on and I sent out chief scout, Ron Yeats, to watch him on two more occasions before we decided to sign him. The fee was £500,000 and he made a very bright start at Liverpool. We played a cup tie at Chesterfield and he looked so comfortable Roy Evans turned to me and said, 'This fellow could be another Mark Lawrenson.' We genuinely thought we had a player who could adapt to the demands of the English game but sadly it did not work out that way. Dean Saunders, then at Aston Villa, gave him a hard time when we lost at Villa Park and Torben very quickly lost his confidence, his head dropped and it became clear he could not handle English-style football. He went home and revived his career to such an extent that he was back in the Danish squad for Euro 96. He was a prime example of a foreign player who failed to get to grips with a different brand of football. He was at his best as a man marker but when we asked him to take on other responsibilities it was too much for him. Some you win and some you lose but when you are the manager your critics only remember the failures. I can vouch for that.

11

The Zipper Club

Allow me to introduce you to one of the most exclusive clubs in the world. Admission is by invitation only and if you don't have the right qualifications you will be turned away. Never in my wildest dreams did I think I would be eligible for automatic membership – especially at the age of 38 – but if you require a heart bypass operation such matters are considered immaterial, and before you know it you are a fully paid-up member.

It is known as the Zipper Club for obvious reasons. They open you up and then they zip you back together when it is all over. Thanks to the advance of medical science it is an operation which is becoming more commonplace and the survival rate has risen considerably over the years. I come from a family with a history of heart disease. My condition had nothing to do with the stress of football or the hectic lifestyle which had become the norm for me ever since I left home at the age of 15 to become a footballer. If it is in your genes you have to accept it and as I discovered later when I spoke to the experts, if you come from a Celtic background you are more susceptible. It was hereditary in my case but when I was told I needed a life-saving operation it still came as an enormous shock. Unbelievable really, although there had been occasions during my playing career when I did not feel 100 per cent. I prided myself on my physical condition and I have been a fitness freak all of my life.

Looking back perhaps I should have been more aware that heart problems had occurred on several occasions in my family. One of my uncles died at the age of 35, and I lost another one when he was in his 40s. My father had the same operation as me but he did not need it until he was 70. From my point of view I found it hard to grasp the idea that I was the latest casualty in the family. I had always believed I was invincible – certainly in a physical sense. I had been a macho man on the pitch and I continued to train just as hard as a manager.

There is such a thing as a fitness bug and I caught it at a young age. Just ten months before I required surgery I had been on holiday in Majorca with a couple of pals and we were burning the candle at both ends. If I was to be diagnosed as having a heart condition it should have been then. Our idea of a holiday was a series of late, boozy nights and frantic exercise to compensate for it the next day. We would spend the morning lounging on the beach, take a break for lunch, and then begin the fitness work. I would swim a mile across the bay and one of the other lads would be waiting for me on the other side with my running shoes. I would then run four miles back to our apartment – up an incline as I remember – with the Mediterranean sun beating down on my head. Back beside the pool we would then do more exercises and sit-ups before going for another night on the town. We hardly slept, we battered our bodies, and we drove ourselves to the limit the next day to repair the damage from the previous evening's escapades. It may sound slightly crazy to most folks but I never thought it was abnormal. I was obsessed with physical fitness but in retrospect I might have died on that holiday because of my heart problem.

But how could I possibly think there was anything wrong with me? I am not looking for sympathy because my illness was curable and the less fortunate do not have that option. Nevertheless it was a hell of a shock to the system when I discovered how serious my condition was.

With hindsight the warning signs had been there. In my mid-20s I suffered more headaches than most players but I tended to shrug them off and bounce back the next day. But as I got older they became worse. It reached the stage where if I had a beer or a glass of wine I would end up with a sore head. I started living on Solpadine. I would take it before I went to bed. I would wake up in the middle of the night with a headache and take some more and then again first thing in the morning. I put it down to my life as a footballer and the stress which presumably came with that.

By the time I got to Rangers I should have realised something was wrong. After I stopped playing and concentrated on the management side I slipped into a regular routine. While the team was warming up on the pitch before a game I would pop into the medical room and have my blood pressure taken. The club doctor would always say the same thing. 'It is a little high but there is nothing to worry about.'

That started to change nine months into my time at Liverpool. By now my blood pressure was classed as very high and I was advised to take an ECG. I went to a clinic in Crosby on Merseyside and they spotted something they were not happy with and asked me to go back the following week for a second test. I know I had dozed off at the clinic and perhaps that alerted them to the thought that I had a potential problem. On the second visit I was put on a treadmill and told few people attained the high level I achieved. This is an exercise designed to get the blood pumping and helps to show if there is any malfunction. I was told that despite my high level of general fitness, there was still something showing. In fact the tests revealed I had suffered a mild heart attack at some stage in my life without even knowing about it. I was shocked when they told me that but I was ready to write it off as part and parcel of the physical side of football.

If you are continually twisting and turning and colliding with other players you think nothing of it when you feel a slight pain in your chest. And I was a physical player who always went in where it hurts. That was the way I played and the very idea I might get injured never crossed my mind.

But that was then and this was now. I was persuaded the next step was to take an angiogram but I tried to forget about that and went home. But it was on my mind and after a few sleepless nights I realised it made sense and went ahead with it. It turned out to be the best decision I ever made but the repercussions in other aspects of my life were also far-reaching.

Try to imagine what was going through my mind when I was told I needed a triple heart bypass operation at the age of 38. Especially a person like me – who had played sport at the highest level for most of my life. I could not dispute medical opinion and was left in no doubt that I needed surgery and the sooner the better. I was told one artery to my heart was 75 per cent blocked, another 85 per cent and a third 90 per cent. If my condition worsened the consequences were potentially fatal.

The penny had finally dropped that I could die at any time without the operation. It might have been a matter of days, weeks or months and when somebody tells you that it pulls you up short. I kept turning the news over in my mind, wondering if I had unwittingly contributed to my own problem because of the way I conducted my life. Yes, it was hectic, unbelievably so in the eyes of some my friends, but I had regarded it as normal. I was told stress increases the chance of a heart attack by pushing up your blood pressure and your heart rate. As the blood flow increases there is a chance that a piece of tissue can break off the artery wall causing a block-age. If you can switch off from time to time you will suffer less stress but I was always on the move. A normal week for me as Liverpool manager involved training with the players five or six days a week, joining in the five-a-sides, attending games and spending other evenings watching other teams. My children were also very important to me. When I was at Rangers they were living in Majorca and I thought nothing of jumping on a plane every week just to spend a Sunday with them before reporting back for work in Glasgow the next day.

When I arrived in Liverpool the family was living in the South of England and I would make quality time to motor down to see them at every opportunity. Yes, it was frantic but I was confident I could handle it. I remember when I told my first wife I was taking the Rangers job I tried to convince her I would not be like other football managers. I said, 'You won't see me working all hours, chewing gum all day and driving myself crazy.' She replied, 'You will be exactly the same as all the other managers' and she was right. Football is my passion but my family comes first in the final analysis and that was why I knew I must have this operation as soon as possible.

The implications began to sink in when Karen came to see me with my young son Jordan. She was bright and bubbly as usual and did not suspect anything was seriously wrong. That made two of us before I had been given the verdict. After the final examination I was expecting the doctor to come in and say, 'Take these pills for a couple of weeks and you will be right as rain.' Wrong. Karen came in to the consulting room and said, 'Well, is everything OK?' I could

126

feel the tears welling up and I asked her to take Jordan out of the room because I did not want him to see his father in an emotional state. Then I told her. This all happened on a Thursday and Liverpool was playing an FA Cup semi-final against Portsmouth at Highbury three days later. I asked the cardiologist when they could perform the operation. He checked with the surgeon and set the date for the following Tuesday. Everything was starting to move very quickly now but I realised I needed to carry on as normal because the Portsmouth game was a massive fixture for Liverpool, and I could not afford to let my personal problems interfere with our preparations. It was essential that I was seen to be working as usual so none of the players would be distracted. Easier said than done perhaps because keeping the lid on something like this was virtually impossible.

Karen must have wondered what she had let herself in for. We had met only a few weeks before and immediately hit it off. I was out to impress her because I had fallen for her in a big way. We had been out on a couple of dates and I felt I had to tell her what was about to happen. I broke the news to her in a restaurant in Sale. There I was, dressed up to the nines in my Versace suede jacket and my designer jeans, looking in pretty good physical shape. I ordered champagne and wondered how she would react when I told her my news. She was the first to know because I could not keep it bottled up in my head any longer. I did worry that she might think it was either some sick joke I was playing on her or I was a bit of a nutter. At this point in our relationship we were still getting to know each other and I did not want her to think there was something weird about me. How would this lovely girl who had come into my life respond when I tried to convince her I was ill? Most people think you are more likely to suffer from heart disease if you are overweight or if you smoke. Neither applied in my case so I was nervous when I told her the situation.

She was totally supportive right from the start, and meeting Karen – she is now my wife – has had a profound effect on the way I conduct myself professionally and privately. I needed all the help I could get from the moment the date for the operation was confirmed. The next few days were a blur and although I am not making excuses for some of the events which subsequently happened I have to admit I was not thinking clearly all the time and anyone who has gone through a similar experience will understand that.

On the Friday the *Sun* newspaper contacted me – the story was obviously beginning to leak – and I foolishly agreed to write an exclusive article about my impending operation. They offered me £50,000 and I accepted although in the end I never took a penny. I planned to have a really good holiday when it was all over and also donate money to charity. In the end Alder Hey Children's Hospital in Liverpool was the only organisation to benefit from that story. When the Hillsborough disaster occurred I was manager of Rangers. In Scotland there is a completely different *Sun* newspaper. It is produced and printed in Glasgow, has its own staff and bears little relation to the version distributed in England. On the sports pages all the football stories concern Scottish clubs and there is little coverage given to what is happening in the Premiership unless there is a major event. Of course the Hillsborough disaster was worldwide news but at that time I was not aware of the depth of feeling against the paper on Merseyside. I had no contact with Liverpool at the time and all I knew about the dreadful events was what I read in the papers. In Scotland there was no mention about the growing anger towards the paper on Merseyside. It may have been given prominence in the English press but in Scotland they concentrated on reporting the facts and aftermath of the tragedy. If I had been better informed I would never have agreed to write that article. This is not an excuse but I think I am entitled to explain the reasons behind my decision to give them that story. Of course I felt for the bereaved families and I would never have deliberately contributed to their sorrow.

The story appeared on a Monday – the day before my operation – and it just went from bad to worse for me after that. It might have been a good idea for me to resign there and then as Liverpool manager. The Cup semi-final had ended in a draw and the replay was on that Monday so I knew I would miss the game. The *Sun* asked me to pose for a picture with Karen in my hospital room to celebrate Liverpool reaching Wembley. I agreed to that but once again fate conspired against me. The replay went to penalties and extra time and the paper missed its deadline. Instead of the picture appearing in the Tuesday edition alongside a report of Liverpool's victory, they decided to hold it over until the next day, 15 April – the anniversary of the Hillsborough disaster. I did not know they were going to do that and if I had known I would have refused them permission to carry the picture. But the damage was done. There were Karen and I smiling out of the page while Liverpool was paying its respects to the 96 people who had died at Hillsborough. The timing could not have been worse and although I was the innocent party over that picture who was going to believe me?

When I contacted the *Sun*'s London office later they admitted it was an unfortunate coincidence. They had overlooked the date of the anniversary and were not aware they were publishing the picture when so many Merseysiders were remembering those lost in Sheffield.

Mike Ellis, my co-writer for this book, could have told them because he was at Hillsborough for the game in 1989, but he was away in America reporting on the World Cup preparations for USA 94 when the unfortunate picture was published and was unaware of what had happened.

It was one mistake after another, but the bottom line is I was responsible for starting it with an ill-judged decision. I did not tell the Liverpool chairmen David Moores or Peter Robinson about the operation until after the game at Highbury was over. On the way back from London I broke the news to the players. Their faces were a study. I think most of them thought it was a wind-up and they found it difficult to take it all in when they realised the full implications.

12

The Operation

When the story appeared in the *Sun* after the game at Highbury it was the signal for a feeding frenzy from the rest of the media. Karen drove me to the Alexandra Hospital in Cheadle where I was to have the operation and there was a big crowd waiting. Television cameras, microphones, photographers and reporters were everywhere waiting to witness my arrival. I asked Karen to drive me away because I needed a little more time to prepare myself. Ten minutes later I said, 'OK, I am ready' and we made our way through the massed ranks of people waiting outside the main entrance.

It is strange what goes through your mind at such a momentous period in your life. I could not forget a remark attributed to one of the Liverpool directors when Karen was caught on television driving my Mercedes on a visit to the hospital. 'What is that woman doing at the wheel of a Liverpool FC vehicle?' It seemed so petty. Well, here was another opportunity for him to criticise me because Karen was the driver again when we arrived at the Alexandra. Who knows why such thoughts pass through your head but along with other examples of the small-minded thinking which permeated most of the Anfield boardroom, it was preoccupying my mind. Perhaps it provided a welcome diversion before the real business of the week began. How anyone could make such a fuss about a minor issue like that was nagging away at me. For the record, we were not exactly short of transport. Karen had her own car but we were jumping in and out of cars so often at that time we never thought anyone would have the gall to take exception to which particular model we were using at a particular time.

There were other occasions when I had witnessed how some members of the board had revealed their lack of maturity. The manager always gets the blame if success proves elusive but the fans should take a closer look at the people with the overall responsibility for running the club. We were discussing proposed economy cuts on one occasion when the suggestion was made we could save money by limiting three new ladies' loos to just one toilet roll between them! Now that would really impress the bank manager. My regular joust at board meetings came with a director named Tony Ensor. I am sure his colleagues fed him some of the ridiculous questions he asked me just to see how I would react. Mr Ensor is a well-known figure in legal circles on Merseyside. At one stage he was a deputy coroner, later the City's recorder and he is now a judge. He was the dominant voice at all the board meetings, always trying to make an impression. I sensed he was unpopular with other members of the board. After several run-ins I began to regard him as a cartoon character. At the end of meetings other directors would privately congratulate me on the way I had handled the latest sparring session. I was convinced he wanted me out of the manager's chair but what he did not realise was the rest of the board were setting him up and in the end he resigned before I did. Much as I disliked him I have to say he was not the person who questioned Karen's right to be driving my club car.

These were the thoughts flashing through my mind as I

prepared for my operation. They would not go away. I remembered another meeting when Terry Smith, a successful businessman who had joined the board, pushed for the need to appoint a top-flight commercial manager for the club. It made sense to me as he outlined the way to go about it. He was proposing we placed an advertisement in the quality Sunday papers, offered however much it would cost to get the best man, and we would reap the benefits. Remember, Liverpool as a brand name in those days was as big as Manchester United, and Terry's argument was the right man would not only pay his way but boost the club's image worldwide. In the end his idea was flattened and the club appointed a local man, Mike Turner, who had been working in rugby league. I don't intend any disrespect to him but it was just another example of how Liverpool were losing their way as the game was entering a boom period. I think the writing was on the wall for them at this time and they have been playing catch-up ever since.

The reality of my own situation soon drove those musings out of my mind once I was in my hospital room. It hit home that all this was for real but the photographers did miss one chance to snatch a picture which I am sure they would have cherished. I had changed into my pyjamas and dressing gown, said goodbye to Karen until she returned later in the day, when she suddenly reappeared because she could not release the immobiliser on the car. I needed to sneak down the fire escape at the back of the hospital and get the car started just a matter of yards away from where the press were assembled. That was one picture which did not make the headlines.

Some people have a fear of hospitals but the vast majority of footballers have undergone various operations at some stage of their careers and accept that surgery is always a possibility. Popping in and out of wards to visit your colleagues or to see football-mad youngsters who are sick becomes a regular part of your life. I have never felt uncomfortable in that environment and I was in comparatively high spirits. I was determined to be the Alexandra's best customer. Later that evening two nurses came into my room and shaved every hair off my body from the neck down. I resembled a plucked chicken. That was when it dawned on me that this was for real. A doctor arrived and ordered me to take off my clothes and get out of bed. He had me standing on a chair and was holding an ordinary felt tip-pen in his hand. He proceeded to mark the inside of my leg in readiness for the operation. That was necessary because they needed to find a vein that could be removed and used in the operation. It was scheduled to last five hours, during which time they would cut through my breastbone and get right to the heart of the matter, if you will excuse the pun. I knew I would be detained for ten days and then face a month's recuperation but I already had the date of 9 July firmly in my mind because I intended to be back at work when Liverpool reported for pre-season training. That gave me three months to make a full recovery and I was confident I could meet that deadline.

Before I settled down to sleep that night, I looked at myself in the mirror and wondered what the next day had in store. I remembered telling my father the previous week: 'I have got some bad news for you. I am going to be a member of your club.' He knew exactly what I was talking about because he had undergone the same operation three years earlier. It could not have been easy for him. Being a parent, there is nothing worse than the possibility of one of your children dying before you. That did not cross my mind because I have never been scared of anything in my life and I felt very positive about the situation.

The Operation

When I woke up after the operation there was no pain whatsoever. I was attached to several tubes and monitors but I felt better each day and I was convinced the worst was over and it would all be plain sailing from then on. But I was too active too soon. I have always been in a rush and I wanted to prove to everybody that not only had I come through this ordeal with flying colours but I was ready to set new records with the speed of my recovery. That was a big mistake. Try getting out of bed without using your arms and you will see how difficult it is. You end up putting your arm on the side of the bed and trying to push yourself up. When you have been cut in half and then put back together again and you are all wired up, the worst possible scenario is to cause movement of your sternum. And that was what I was doing in my eagerness to accelerate my progress. It was a weird feeling to feel a click inside your chest whenever you moved. You did not hear it but you felt it and the medical staff were most unhappy when I informed them what I was experiencing.

I was trying too hard and I paid for it. I had a neat little scar on my chest after the operation but by the end of the week it began to weep. The hospital did not show any concern about that and I was still feeling fine. Friends were coming to visit from Scotland and Liverpool, Karen was bringing me my favourite Italian food and everything seemed to be progressing smoothly. But the weeping from my scar was beginning to increase. From being a tiny hole, it grew until it was big enough to fit a golf ball inside. If I was lying down the fluid would trickle out. If I sat up it was like turning a tap on – it just flowed from my body. It looked like milky tea and I did not know what I had done to cause this setback. I was put on a new series of drugs to combat the infection but I was still determined to leave hospital after ten days.

The media had been camped out from day one and I agreed

135

with my doctors that I would give a brief press conference when I was discharged. My intention was to allow them to take their pictures, ask a few questions, and then I wanted them to leave me alone so I could convalesce in peace. The night before I was due to be discharged I began to feel ill for the first time.

I remember getting up in the early hours to go the toilet and feeling dizzy. I fell over on the way back to my bed and that was the start of serious problems. An infection was racing through my body. I was having trouble breathing and one of my lungs was filling up with fluid. My mother had died of emphysema and I recalled how distressing it had been to watch her when she needed oxygen to relieve her condition. My symptoms were similar and I pleaded with the nurses to do something. They were always brilliant to me with a smile and a joke whenever they came into my room. They were experts at keeping a patient's spirits high and I have nothing but admiration for the work they do. Certainly I could not have been in better hands and I was always grateful for their kind attention. They never stop working yet always find the time to talk to you despite their heavy workload. Nothing is too much trouble. No wonder the country at large holds them in such esteem – you can add my name to the list after the way they cared for me.

When I became agitated they tried to reassure me that I was OK and just excited at the prospect of going home in the morning. But I could not breathe properly and I was getting anxious. Eventually I was given oxygen and my discharge date was cancelled. For the next few days I knew what feeling really ill was all about. The cardiologist was baffled by this development and thought an embolism was a possibility. The worry now was that the infection might spread into my sternum. My condition deteriorated and breathing was becoming increasingly difficult. Karen was with me all the time and often stayed overnight at the Alexandra. I remember there were doctors and a couple of nurses in my room on one occasion and I begged them to do something. I did not know what was happening to me and the medical staff seemed unsure of what to do. For the first time I began to wonder if I might not pull through.

I could see Karen standing by the wall with tears streaming down her face when the doctors went into a huddle for a private conversation. She probably knew more about what was going on than I did and she told me later that there was an air of panic about my condition. The decision was taken to drain the fluid from my lung.

That is a pretty basic procedure. Not to put too fine a point on it you are literally stabbed in the back and rubber tubing is inserted inside you. That did not hurt but when they started drawing the fluid from my lung it was the most painful experience of my life. I was screaming out loud as the fluid was drawn from my body, and I went through that routine three times before they had completed the task. For the first time I really thought I might die. I was lying on my side while they drained me and I could see Karen standing by the wall. There was a plastic container behind me which kept filling up and Karen could see everything that was happening. In a sense it was worse for her because although I could feel the pain I could not see what they were doing to me and she could. She told me later the fluid was pouring out of me and they had to keep stopping to empty the container. It must have been a horrific spectacle for her to witness and it all became too much for her. Suddenly her legs gave way and she slowly slipped to the floor and put her head in her hands and cried her eyes out. It was a harrowing time; unforgettable for all the wrong reasons.

This complication meant a second operation. I needed to be opened up again and have my wound cleaned out. Then I was back in intensive care feeling weaker than ever. My breathing remained a problem and I was no longer feeling so sure of myself. I went for X-rays every day and I did not even have the strength to get myself out of bed. I was incapable of washing myself. Just cleaning my teeth was sufficient to make me feel tired. For five days I could do nothing. If I needed a shower I would be helped into the bathroom and placed on a stool because I was not strong enough to stand up. I lost around two stone in weight and when I look at the pictures of how I was then I must have been crazy to have even contemplated going to the Cup Final. I just felt I had to be there and although the doctors did not veto the idea they were not exactly keen on it either. Wembley was always at the back of my mind but we shall return to that later.

Apart from the physical trauma from such a major operation I was about to discover there were other significant side-effects which would test my resolve. They changed me as a person and brought home to me that I could be vulnerable just like anyone else. Unless I had experienced those events for myself I would never have believed I could feel so low emotionally, and it coloured the way I changed my outlook on life – I think for the better. Thank goodness I had Karen for support. When we first met we were both basically lonely people. There was an instant chemistry between us and within a matter of weeks of meeting her I was thinking of buying her a ring. Our relationship became rock solid in a very short space of time and she became my indispensable support – and I surely needed somebody to help me.

When I was recovering from my second operation I foolishly believed the worst was over because nobody had warned me you could also suffer mentally in the aftermath of life-saving surgery. I knew I was weak physically and it would take me a long time to recover my strength but I never anticipated how the operation would affect me in other ways. The repercussions went on for a long time and made me realise there is much more to life than just feeling good and looking fit. In fact it means very little in the broader context but you must understand I had a different view before my medical problems were diagnosed.

I had always regarded myself as untouchable when it came to physical health. Even when I stopped playing I continued to train as hard as ever. I worked every day with the players on the pitch and in the gym and when I went home I used the facilities at a nearby health club before finishing with a sauna. That was my routine and as much a part of my life as having breakfast every morning. I was very conscious about my diet and I intended to rebuild my life on the same lines once my body regained its strength. The very idea that I might suffer mental anguish just did not register. Wrong again, Souness, and another remainder that you are never too old to learn that there are a few twists and turns you can never anticipate – no matter how clever you think you are.

If anyone had suggested I might fall victim to a panic attack I would have laughed in their face. But it happened and I have never felt so helpless. A man who did not know the meaning of the word fear was suddenly reduced to a frightened man, terrified that he would be unable to find his way back to his hospital room. At this stage I was on the mend and due to be discharged in a couple of days.

I felt I was ready for some gentle exercise and went for a walk in the hospital grounds. The media were still camped out at the hospital so I went through the back door and along a path which led to some woods. I became adventurous and was not aware of how far I had walked although it was not a problem, because if I looked back I could see the Alexandra. I decided to take a short-cut back and came off the path. I was in the trees at this point but confident I was heading in the right direction. Then I came to a fence and I knew I could not climb it. That was when I began to worry. I thought if I fell over now nobody would ever find me and I suffered a panic attack. It was a new experience for me. It may sound silly but to me it was very serious. I was the guy who had spent his life confronting anything that came my way. I had always met any challenge head on. Nothing fazed me. I could handle anything and now suddenly I could not cope with a simple situation and it alarmed me. I tried to tell myself to calm down and concentrate on finding the path again but I was shocked at how helpless I felt. Eventually I got back to my room but I was badly shaken by the whole episode and it was another warning that I had a long way to go before I was back to my normal self.

There were other incidents which undermined my morale and left me wondering if I ever would be the same person again. I was worried and racked by self-doubt and it brought me to a low threshold just when I thought I was on the road to recovery.

There were nights in hospital when I would wake up saturated in a cold sweat. That was the result of so much anaesthetic being pumped into my system for the two operations I had undergone in the space of ten days. On one occasion I needed my bedding changed six times in one night. I would be soaking with body sweat. Eventually I became so tired I did not want to disturb the night staff any more so I would just lie there shivering until the morning. I was cold, wet and miserable. One part of the bed was warm and dry and the other soaking. It was that way for a while when I returned home and I was beginning to realise there was more to this than just the mechanics of the operation.

There were instances of how far I had slipped when Karen and I went on holiday to America after the Cup Final. I had been told that the air in Phoenix, Arizona, would be good for me and an ideal place to aid my recovery. The advice was correct. It was a wonderful place and we were based in a superb hotel. But I could not escape from what I perceived as more embarrassment. At the airport as we waited for our baggage to arrive at the carousel I felt people were talking about me because I was asking a porter to lift our luggage off and transport it to a cab. Although I had lost a lot of weight I still looked in reasonable condition to people who did not know me and I was convinced they were thinking, 'Who does this guy think he is?' The truth was I did not have the strength to carry my own luggage and the same thing happened when we arrived at the hotel. I asked a bell boy to unload it and was acutely aware that anyone watching would think I was some phoney big shot who could not be bothered to soil his hands. I only wished I had been capable of carrying a few suitcases because it would have been a sign that I was improving.

In Phoenix it came home to me how weak I was and it produced a minor row with Karen. I was lying in bed half-asleep one morning when she dressed for a workout in the hotel's health centre. She was in her gym gear ready to go when I started to cry. 'What is the matter?' she asked. The only other time she had seen me cry was when my father died. This time I felt so helpless because she was healthy and ready to enjoy some exercise and I was in bed feeling sorry for myself. I cannot emphasise how much care and attention Karen gave me at this time but I also have to admit that it hurt me to see her on the way to the gym when I felt so useless.

There were other days when I would wake in tears but

what I did not realise at the time was that this was a natural reaction to my operation. When we returned to England I asked the doctors about it and they said most patients go through this phase once they have recovered from surgery. I just wish they had warned me about it in the first place so I would have been prepared. Karen assured me that I had handled the operation well and that she had been told many patients suffered from depression but that had not happened in my case. There were low points but they did not persist. Again she was my prop, constantly encouraging me and raising my spirits and she got me back in the gym sooner than I could have expected.

13

The 1992 Cup Final

I must have been crazy to attend the 1992 Cup Final in May but I felt it was my duty to be there for a number of reasons. I knew I was not well – I only had to look in the mirror to realise that – but I was the manager of Liverpool and at least I was back on my feet so I was determined to get to the game one way or another. I was required to give the medical staff certain guarantees that I would not over tax myself. I knew they had reservations about me going to London and would have been happier if I had stayed away. Perhaps it was my old stubborn streak emerging again, but after what I had gone through I was mobile again and it was time to face the music.

I flew down from Manchester to Heathrow and caught a taxi to the team hotel outside St Albans. It must have been a first in the history of the FA Cup when the manager of one of the teams makes his own way down to London with nobody to keep him company. It was a strange feeling when I walked into the team hotel. They were in safe hands with Ronnie Moran in command and I felt like an outsider looking in. I was never going to lead them out of the Wembley tunnel and I was trying to adopt a low profile because I did not want to be a distraction so near to the game. To be honest I was

exhausted when I reached the hotel. I was purposely travelling light but even the effort of carrying a small case left me
feeling weak. I had learned my lesson after the second operation and was determined to take every precaution to avoid
a repeat of the problems I experienced when I tried to do too
much too soon.

It may seem unusual for somebody in my condition to
make that journey on his own but at that stage I was alone
as far as the club was concerned. After all the fuss about the
Sun article the club had been keeping their distance. The
chairmen David Moores and Peter Robinson were conspicu-
ous by their absence until my final days in hospital. I could
understand that. I had placed them in a difficult position but
some moral support would have been appreciated. However,
it was not to be so I went solo. It was my duty to be at
Wembley to judge for myself the feedback I received from the
Liverpool fans. One option I was considering was to resign
after the game if I was given a hostile reception. When I was
in hospital they kept the newspapers away from me but I was
aware I had inflamed feelings on Merseyside, because Karen
kept me up to date about what was being written about me.

I deliberately stayed in the tunnel as the players made
their way on to the pitch and I was trying to be as discreet as
possible. I walked around the pitch perimeter to the
Liverpool bench while the preliminaries were taking place
and I have to say I was not aware of anything negative being
directed towards me. I was waiting for it and would not have
been surprised it if had happened. I was expecting criticism
but in all honesty I did not hear any and I was super sensitive that day and anticipating the worst.

Liverpool won the game but I did not celebrate with the
players and the coaching staff. Karen had come down on the
Friday night and after the match we went back to our hotel,

ordered room service and I was in bed by 8 p.m. I did get all the newspapers delivered on Sunday morning because I wanted to know how my appearance at the game had been reported. There were a few nasty shocks when I the saw verdict of the press. Strangely, only one newspaper claimed a section of the Liverpool fans booed me when I appeared out of the tunnel. If that was the case why did not all the papers write something similar? The one person who wrote that used to be a friend of mine. When I was a player at Liverpool I would often spend time with him on foreign trips and I thought he was a journalist I could trust. Why of all people did he see fit to write something like that when my so-called enemies in the press did not?

I knew there would be some journalists waiting for something to happen and they would have milked it just to hammer me again. Another paper alleged I had gone to Wembley determined to steal the limelight. That hurt because I was still low at the time and the whole day became a personal ordeal and quite stressful. As I mentioned earlier, I needed to be there for all sorts of reasons, but the last thing on my mind was to bask in any reflected glory if Liverpool won the Cup. That was not why I was there. And just for the record I gave my Cup medal to one of the players who was not in the team at Wembley. I don't possess an FA Cup medal. I have all the others in my collection but I did not think it would be right to keep the 1992 medal in those circumstances.

My relationship with the press had become difficult after the *Sun* story. I knew most of the sports writers on Merseyside from my time as a player but I did not go out of my way to give them special treatment. My philosophy was to treat everyone the same way but some of them tried to make it a closed shop and explained how they had worked with Kenny Dalglish. They wanted to keep that system in place but I was prepared to give access to all sections of the media and see how they treated me before I thought about excluding anyone.

Once I had given the *Sun* an exclusive, the situation changed dramatically. I can understand other newspapers trying to retaliate but some of the stuff written about me went well over the top. I think I have a thick skin and can take most things thrown at me but some of the comments did upset me. I have never claimed to be everybody's cup of tea but it made me take stock and have a fresh look at myself. It was a humbling experience. Humble was the last word you would find in my vocabulary, but it was surfacing. I realised I must have upset an awful lot of people down the years without even being aware of it. I am not referring to the *Sun* episode here but other instances. As a footballer I knew I was not popular outside my own club because of the way I played the game. But that was different. On the field of play it does not matter what the opposition think of you. It is all about winning and I admit I did not take many prisoners. My own team mates had a nickname for me – Champagne Charlie, and before every game Phil Neal used to say to me, 'Make sure they are all jumping today, Charlie.'

I was being judged as an individual – not as a sportsman – and some of the comments were so personal it did make me wonder if I was the loathsome creature some people would have you believe. I had to admit that in the eyes of most of the public I must have come across as a really horrible person and that was a shock. I hope I am mistaken but it seemed a classic case of hitting a man when he is down. I was far from well, mentally and physically I was at a low ebb and those body blows did hit home.

Things had obviously changed when we started the

1992–93 season and it soon became apparent that I no longer enjoyed the full support of the board. My first concern was how the players would react and I have to be fair to them – they never caused me a problem over the issue. It would have been easy for some of them to make the most of the opportunity but it never happened. The previous season I had been particularly hard on some of the senior pros who I felt had not been pulling their weight but I certainly did not sense any hostility in the dressing room when we began pre-season training. Upstairs, the circumstances had changed and my old friend Tony Ensor sensed this was the time to strike.

Although we had won the FA Cup, we had finished sixth in the Premiership which was not good enough by Liverpool standards. The Cup success meant we had changed a poor season into one that was just about acceptable but of course with the article in the *Sun* I had blotted my copy-book and Mr Ensor was not about to let me forget it. I knew my backing inside the boardroom had diminished considerably. They wanted to step back and ensure nobody could accuse them of offering wholehearted support to the manager. Mistakenly I thought we could get over my indiscretion and with a place in Europe secure I was anticipating a much better season.

Tony Ensor did not worry me but I should have realised there and then that my relations with the board would never be the same again. The meetings would last an hour and I am sure they provided plenty of amusement for the other directors as Mr Ensor fired a stream of irrelevant questions in my direction. He always tried to dominate the proceedings. David Moores was the chairman but he rarely opened his mouth on these occasions. Mr Ensor finally signed his own death warrant by giving them an ultimatum: either the manager goes or I do. He went.

If that was a signal that the rest of the board was prepared to back me I cannot say I was convinced. David Moores was forever telling me we were mates but I felt he could have done more to indicate that to the fans. And let us be honest, they must have been wondering how the club would handle the situation. I don't think David knows what a true friend is and it is not all his fault. When you are a member of the Littlewoods family and brought up in a such a privileged position it is only natural to be wary. As a young man I am sure he learned that lesson. There are many hangers-on out there eager to jump on the back of a rich man and enjoy the ride. The world is full of rip-off merchants and David is such an easy-going guy he would be an obvious target for a conman who could have fleeced him unless he was on his guard. It is sad but I think a natural suspicion of people trying to get too close to him has stayed with him.

I understood his position but he was the chairman of Liverpool and he was employing me as the manager. These were difficult times for the club, but if he really believed in me I think I was entitled to hear a few words of encouragement uttered beyond the confines of the boardroom, and I am not alluding to the traditional chairman's vote of confidence which normally precedes the chop.

David would ring me late at night worried about which direction the club was taking but the next day if I saw him at Anfield our previous conversation would never be mentioned. Don't get me wrong. I don't dislike him as a man and anyone who has come into contact with him will understand what I am saying. He is the football fan who became the chairman of his favourite club. I don't believe he wanted to deal with the day-to-day problems which come with the job. He just wanted to be there on match day and watch his beloved Liverpool team win. Yes, he cares and he has demonstrated that by pouring millions of pounds into the club but I have to

©MSI

Returning to Anfield. Here I am with Ronnie Moran.

Two early signings: Dean Saunders (left) and Mark Wright.

©ALLSPORT

In the hot seat with Liverpool. To the right of me are Phil Boersma and Roy Evans. *(Above)*

I stand to make a point. *(Right)*

Even though it was soon after my heart operation, I was determined to make it to the FA Cup Final in 1992 against Sunderland.

The Liverpool team celebrate our 2-0 win over Sunderland at Wembley.

As manager of Galatasaray, taking the team's flag to plant it in the pitch of rivals Fenerbahce after a famous Cup win. It caused quite a reaction.

With Lawrie McMenemy at Southampton. *(Above)*

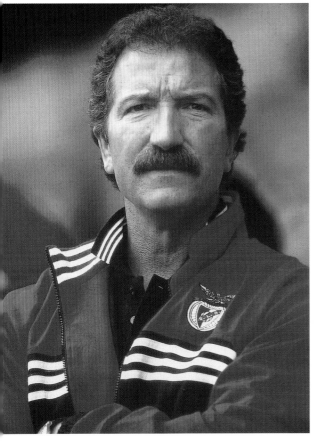

As manager of Benfica. *(Left)*

I brought Dean Saunders to Benfica – the third time that I have managed him to date.

With my wife, Karen, at our wedding in Las Vegas in 1994.

With Karen, and (l-r) Fraser, Daniel and Lauren.

say he did not conform to the stereotype of a Premiership chairman.

At Rangers I worked with David Holmes and David Murray and I knew I could rely on them to back me whenever necessary. They were prepared to speak out to the media but David Moores is rarely quoted in the newspapers. I understand that he is happy for Peter Robinson to take charge of running the club but these were exceptional circumstances and I think the Liverpool supporters were waiting for him to say something about the situation. It never happened. It was as though he felt if he kept his head down with a bit of luck the whole business would go away and we could carry on as usual.

But at a club the size of Liverpool that was wishful thinking. Roy Evans was promoted as my assistant because he was rightly regarded as a nice guy and the thinking was he could counter my more abrasive approach. I did not see the change as a threat to my own position but it is ironic that after four years in the job Roy left with his critics claiming he had been too soft on the players. Oh for the happy balance – sometimes you wonder if you can ever win in this game.

I am sure in his way David Moores did think we were great mates, but our definition of what constitutes a genuine friendship is clearly different. My idea of a mate is somebody who is prepared to stand shoulder to shoulder with you when he is needed. That is what I would do if a pal of mine ever needed help. If anyone said anything critical about somebody close to me I would be the first to respond. I never felt I had that from David Moores. I would have appreciated it if he had come to me privately and said he could not make a public statement in my defence after what had happened but I should know he was right behind me. I knew it was a tricky situation but I felt entitled to more than I received from him.

There was plenty of informal chat when he was quick to emphasise how well we hit it off but that great friendship has never extended to him once picking up the telephone to talk to me since I left the club. I never fell out with David and you could argue that he was new to the role of chairman but how long does it take to learn the ropes of being a mate?

With the problems behind the scenes perhaps it was not surprising that we had an indifferent season on the pitch in 1992–93. Players and fans can sense when everything is not as it should be, and they say that when it comes down to football Liverpool is a like a village and everyone knows the latest gossip. We finished sixth again in the Premiership but our Cup form deserted us. We went out of the Cup-Winners' Cup in the second round to a very good Spartak Moscow side, not helped by some bizarre goalkeeping from Bruce Grobbelaar which culminated in him being sent off. I got into trouble with the referee too. Little Chesterfield gave us an almighty fright in the League Cup when they drew 4–4 at Anfield before we went through in the replay, but we did not last much longer and were beaten by Crystal Palace in the next round. Most damaging of all was our failure to get beyond the first hurdle in our defence of the FA Cup. We scraped a 2–2 draw at Bolton before losing 2–0 at Anfield. A year later a similar result at the same stage of the competition turned out to be my swansong as Liverpool manager.

14

The Leaving of Liverpool

At the start of the 1993–94 season the pressure was growing for Liverpool to re-establish themselves as one of the game's dominant forces and I knew my position as manager was under the microscope. Finishing sixth again was not acceptable by many people's standards. I was still recuperating and the mental trauma of my operation had changed me. Physically I was on the mend but an incident during the early part of the previous season had made me wonder if I was the same person. It was important to project a positive attitude and keep any doubts to myself but I could not forget what had happened when we had played Aston Villa twelve months earlier.

Ron Atkinson is an old friend of mine and we had arranged to have a night out after the match. Karen was motoring down to Birmingham to meet me and Ron's wife, Maggie. We lost the match 4–2, Dean Saunders scored twice for Villa, and Ronny Rosenthal hit the bar from two yards out for Liverpool. It was an amazing miss and earned him the dubious distinction of being featured in a video which recorded the worst misses of all time. Liverpool had slumped to 17th place in the Premiership after just nine games. It was a bad day whichever way you looked at it and the lowest

I had ever felt in a footballing environment. I was totally depressed and it crossed my mind that I might never again be the strong forceful character that I had been before the operation.

I sat in Ron's office after the game trying to collect my thoughts but I was being engulfed by a black mood – a new and potentially worrying situation for me. Ron is always upbeat – win or lose – because he has the right philosophy for this job. He was trying to jolly me along but when I left the ground I knew I would be miserable company on what should have been a relaxing night out with Karen and some good friends. Ron was leading the way towards the hotel with me following behind. I flashed my headlights for him to stop and told him I could not go out for dinner. He tried to change my mind but by then I was feeling worse than ever. Ron argued that we all lose games and next week it would be my turn to be a winner while he might be feeling down but I just could not face the prospect of trying to put on a brave face. Nobody enjoys good food and wine more than me but the manner of our defeat had got to me and I needed to be on my own. I telephoned Karen on my mobile to inform her of my change of plan even though she was on the outskirts of Birmingham by then.

I turned the car around and headed up the M6 for Knutsford and I cried all the way home. I had tears streaming down my face on the 80-mile journey and goodness knows what other motorists would have made of that if they had recognised me. I was in bed by eight and seriously questioning whether I was strong enough, mentally and physically, for such a demanding job. Suddenly it came home to me that all the events leading up to the 1992 FA Cup Final had taken a bigger toll that I realised.

I felt like Mr Average. I wondered if the op had the same

effect on others who had gone through the same experience. I was no longer the man who could handle anything that came his way. Tears came easily on other occasions, apart from the Villa episode, and I feared my personality might be undergoing a dramatic change. I was worried and felt vulnerable for the first time in my life. The only person I could confide in was Karen. I don't know how I would have coped without her. She assured me I would be OK and it was inevitable there would be some side-effects.

For the 1993–94 season I had appointed Ian Rush as captain. It was a move designed to heal the breach between us. When I was a Liverpool player he was the best finisher in the game, a natural, and his goal return was phenomenal. At his peak he was untouchable but when I returned as manager we fell out. I felt I was not getting his full support at a time when I really needed it. He had never made any secret of his displeasure when I substituted him in games but I needed him and Liverpool needed him. He was still capable of getting his 20 goals a season and this was the time to put aside personal feelings in the interests of the team. He remained a crowd favourite and I thought the captain's armband was the clearest indication I could give him that he still had a major role to play.

Rushie was instrumental in the development of Robbie Fowler. When I first suggested to the backroom staff that we give Robbie his chance in a League Cup tie against Fulham they were all against it. He was 17 and although they recognised his potential they did not think he had the maturity to perform at the highest level at such a young age. Rushie had taken a shine to Robbie when he first joined the club and taken him under his wing. Robbie idolised him, so it all made sense to me. Whatever my differences with Rushie during my time as manager I would be the first to give him credit for helping in Robbie's rapid rise. He would take time to talk him through what was required from a front-line striker and Robbie was always prepared to listen. I have remarked in another chapter how disappointed I was by the lack of support the senior pros showed to the emerging players but I could not fault Rushie for his help in nurturing Fowler's talent.

It was a difficult season. We were not in European competition, and at the half-way stage we were off the pace for the title. There was worse to come in the New Year when we were drawn away to Bristol City in the FA Cup. A disturbing comment attributed to one of my players had been passed down the line to me at this stage and it was a clear indication that there could be trouble ahead. A local journalist had pointed out the fact that we faced three crucial games – including the visit of Manchester United – all in a short period and these fixtures could determine how our season unfolded. I have no reason to doubt the word of the person who related this tale to me but the response he received from this very experienced player was, 'Maybe it won't be such a bad thing if we lose all of them.'

The writing was on the wall. Defeats could hasten my departure and that would suit this individual. How many others felt the same way? I won't name names here but that player was in the side knocked out by Bristol City because I still believed he could make a meaningful contribution, especially as we were playing at home. He was a regular in the side and continued to be after I had left. I hope he can look me in the eye if we meet again. The upshot of all this was that the divisions in the camp were growing wider and I was becoming more of an isolated figure.

Before we went to Bristol we drew with Manchester United at Anfield, coming back from a three goal deficit which suggested we could still raise our game against the big boys. But how would we approach a potential banana skin in the shape of Bristol City? That was part of the problem. Yes, the team could lift itself against our biggest rivals, but could I trust them to do the same in a knockout competition? The reader can rightly point the finger in my direction because this was my team and even I could not rely on them from one game to another. That was how far the situation had degenerated.

I should have known the omens were not good for that Cup tie. A couple of days before the game I had a crown fitted at the dentist and on the way to the game it became loose. I wondered then if that was a precursor for what was to follow. The first game was abandoned when the floodlights failed with the score at 1–1. When we tried again the playing surface was atrocious and we scraped another draw, but Bristol had seen enough of us by then to know they had a good chance of causing an upset, even at Anfield. Russell Osman, their manager, confirmed that when, quite by chance, I was able to listen in to his team talk before the replay. It comes to something when your worst fears are confirmed literally out of the mouth of your next opponent!

We had reported to our hotel on the afternoon of the game and I was having my tea and toast around 4.30, not realising that Bristol City had reserved a suite next to my room for their team talk – and I could hear every word that was said. I mean no disrespect to Russell Osman or Bristol City but they were a First Division club coming to Anfield to face Liverpool and that should have been sufficient to have them on edge. Don't you believe it. I could hear Russell assessing my players on an individual basis and I thought to myself, 'That is exactly the way I would describe them.' He was spot on. The main thrust of his argument was, 'If you go out and match Liverpool for effort they will throw in the towel.'

This was my team he was talking about and I was shocked that others perceived us in this way. The longer the game progressed the more I realised how accurate his preparation had been. I knew that night I was wasting my time trying to produce the Liverpool team that the fans craved. I had lost the support of the players – they were not performing for me – and it was time to call it a day. An outsider had described my team in exactly the same terms I would have used myself. It brought home the reality that when it came to a physical cup tie we were no longer up for it, and that was the biggest crime of all. We lost the game 1–0 and I knew my time was up. If Bristol City knew how to beat us in our own back yard I thought it must be common knowledge through-out the game that this Liverpool team was a spent force.

The day after the game I asked for a meeting with David Moores. It took place at his house and Peter Robinson also attended with the former chairman Sir John Smith. I told them I intended to resign and asked them to pay up the remainder of my contract. I did not feel embarrassed making that demand and I pointed out that Liverpool had originally enticed me away from Rangers where I had a job for life. Peter asked me to reconsider and although there had been an occasion before when he had talked me out of quitting, I knew there was no turning back this time. Peter was always my strongest ally in the boardroom and I appreciated his support but in the chairman's house I made it clear to them the job had become untenable because I was not getting the full support of the players. When that happens a manager's job becomes impossible. You are there to be shot at when results go wrong and whether it is your fault or not becomes immaterial. We are living in the age of player power and managers and coaches have to understand that. The big stick no longer works when players are in the millionaire bracket.

I reflected on the squad I had inherited and will always maintain that the odds were stacked against me from the start. The squad had required major surgery before I arrived. Too many players were past their sell-by date and there was little coming through the ranks – certainly nobody who was ready to step straight into the senior team. When money becomes more important than pride and passion a manager's ranting and raving makes little impression. Players who reach the top cannot lose. A watertight contract protects them. They cannot be sacked and they cannot resign. The only way out is if they retire, and they are not going to do that unless injury or old age determines their future. Managers are disposable; even more so in the modern game. I could have stayed on because Liverpool did not intend to sack me but circumstances had conspired against me in such a manner I felt I could not take Liverpool any further. I remembered the glory days the club had enjoyed over the previous three decades and I did feel a sense of failure. Whatever the faults of the current team, the bottom line is that the manager must take the responsibility. That is the way it works in this business and if I had chosen to carry on it would have been to the detriment of the club. Overall the fans had been patient. Naturally there was a growing voice of dissent but they had not turned on me in a hostile manner. Liverpool fans love their club more than any individual and although they knew everything was not right, their support for the men in red never wavered.

I am told they are more critical these days and the team has even been booed off the pitch at Anfield. I don't remember that happening in my time, but that was years ago and apart from one League Cup success the cupboard has

remained bare. Presumably that is why they are now beginning to show their impatience. As I have said in a previous
chapter, the club was already in decline when I was
appointed. My biggest regret was I failed to halt that. Roy
Evans spent heavily to try and turn things around and now
it is Gerard Houllier's task. I wish him well but I don't know
if the great days will ever return for Liverpool. The bright
lights of London attract the top foreign players and with
Liverpool out of Europe what do they have to offer as an
alternative? An occasional Cup Final appearance is no
compensation for the failure to win a championship and you
need to go back to 1989–90 for the last time Liverpool
managed that. When you think how much success they
enjoyed over a 30-year period I think it is remarkable that
the fans have remained so loyal through the barren times,
filling Anfield to capacity and making them second only to
Manchester United for the size of their support. If Anfield
was as big as Old Trafford who knows what the average
attendance would be?

The majority of those supporters can remember the
wonderful European nights when their club was rightly
hailed as the best club side this country has ever produced.
It was all about Manchester United in the 1998–99 season
but they have some way to go to match Liverpool's record of
four European Cup triumphs. Those memories burn bright
inside me too, so I was just as frustrated as them. The big
difference was that I had been presented with the opportunity to put it right and history will show I failed. If you
believe everything you hear I was responsible for much more
than that. I had been accused of trying to change the training routines, demolishing the famous bootroom and introducing draconian methods which shook the club to its foundations.

Whenever the decline of Liverpool is discussed, my name usually gets a mention but anyone who looks at it with an unbiased eye will realise that the charges against me were nonsense. Bill Shankly laid down the training methods when he arrived in 1959 and they became admired all over the world. The top coaches from abroad were beating a path to Melwood to observe, learn and digest the secrets of Liverpool's success. The same people, headed by Ronnie Moran, were still preaching the Shankly way when I returned. It is true I did want to introduce some new ideas but nothing that would radically change the Liverpool way. I respected Ronnie as a coach. The club was his life. He was an established player in the team even before Shankly arrived and it was a natural progression for him to join the coaching staff when his playing career ended.

But the game was moving on and I encountered some resistance when I tried to change some of the old ways. In retrospect perhaps I should have been stronger and insisted we implemented my ideas but I was also aware that the Shankly system had been responsible for laying the foundations for everything that followed on. Looking back I now realise the Liverpool job came too early for me. I am a more experienced manager now and I have learned from some of the mistakes made at Anfield. When I went to Rangers the club had endured ten years without winning anything. I was given a free hand to do it my way with the full backing of first David Holmes and then David Murray. Fortunately we won the championship in my first year and we were on our way. We did not win it the following season but three more titles followed in succession after that.

At Rangers I was allowed to make the changes I felt were necessary but at Liverpool it was different. It was hard to persuade them to change anything. If I was guilty of anything, it was accepting that the old ways were still the best. I should have imposed my own ideas and demanded my methods were accepted. I did not and contributed to my own downfall.

As a player I had always enjoyed training under Ronnie. He knew I put everything into it and that was the way he liked it. If you are happy in your work it shows, and I was his type of player. He always picked me for his five-a-side team along with Phil Neal, Jimmy Case and Ray Kennedy. We never lost. It may have helped that Ronnie was also the referee as well as being on our side. Kenny Dalglish would get the occasional game in our team but he was a terrible five-a-side player!

I was blamed for making Melwood our full-time head-quarters. To me that was just common sense. For years the players had always reported to Anfield, changed into their training gear, and been bussed down to Melwood. But there had been many changes at Anfield. A club shop had been opened, a museum was planned, and it was always busy. There was much more traffic in and out of the place, with hundreds of kids waiting to catch a glimpse of their heroes. In addition, car parking space was very limited and there was every possibility of an accident occurring and somebody being hurt. Anfield was expanding at a rapid rate and the club was encouraging people to use its corporate facilities on a daily basis.

Restaurants were being built, seminars were being staged and there were even afternoon tea dances. You can get married at Anfield these days. It all represented the changing face of football. Once stadiums only came to life when the team was playing but clubs were realising that the commercial aspect of running a club was becoming increasingly more important. Football was in fashion and it was only natural that the clubs should seek to take advantage of that.

All the big clubs in Europe had a training area away from the stadium. Some of them had accommodation so it became more than a work place. Some players lived on the premises. I wanted Melwood to be built on those lines with proper dressing rooms, a medical centre and a canteen. We could work in privacy, have the space we needed, and none of the distractions which we faced at Anfield. It seemed a logical step to me. Since then Liverpool has built a multi-million pound youth academy on the outskirts of the city, which does have living quarters as well as state-of-the-art facilities to promote the development of young players. So I don't think I was proposing anything radical when I moved everything to Melwood, but it was still opposed in some quarters.

Diet was another issue. It has become an integral part of a professional footballer's life. In the old days the Liverpool team coach would stop on the way home from an away trip and everyone would be handed fish and chips wrapped in newspaper. Now it is all about eating healthy food, with pasta at the top of the menu. This did not just apply at Liverpool; all clubs were becoming aware that the modern game demanded that players become more responsible. They need to be athletes and a sensible diet has become an essential part of their lives. Years ago they would enjoy the luxury of a three-month summer break. Many would report back for pre-season training overweight and out of condition. Now the close season is contracting every year and six weeks is the maximum they are away from the training ground. Players are also expected to keep themselves fit during their holidays so when they do report back they are in reasonable shape.

As for the bootroom, it was a club decision to demolish it.

The ground was being renovated and more space was required to expand the press room. That certainly did not come within the manager's brief but because it happened during my time I was saddled with the blame. Why on earth would I want to see the end of such a famous Liverpool shrine?

When it was all over I did not attend the press conference on the Friday to announce my resignation. Instead Karen and I left for a short holiday in the South of France. I was not trying to dodge the issue but I was not in the mood to face some of the journalists who I knew would welcome my departure and I could just picture them with a smirk on their faces. I did not need that. It was my decision to leave so why should I give them the satisfaction of answering their questions? In a sense they had got what they wanted when I walked out.

The previous season a lunch had been arranged in an attempt to improve relations with the press. It was held in an Italian restaurant and was all very civilised. The wine had been flowing and that is sometimes when you hear the truth. Colin Wood of the *Daily Mail* was somebody I had got on well with as a player. At this lunch he was anxious to repair our relationship and build some bridges which was fine with me. But I realised nothing had changed when he blurted out he could never forgive me for the article in the *Sun*. We were back to square one and he was off my Christmas card list after that. He was not the only one either, but they were all present in the restaurant when he said it. When I first became manager the journalists who I had known when I was a player expected to get preferential treatment because of our previous association but my relationship with most of them turned sour after the *Sun* article. There were a few I still trusted but they were the minority. The rest were looking to damn me in print at every opportunity.

Well, now they could have a field-day because I had left. In the next five years I set foot in Liverpool on only five occasions – and two of those were to attend funerals.

15

Over the Garden Wall

For the first time in 23 years I was out of football. Ever since I signed for Tottenham at the age of 15 it had been my life but I was pleasantly surprised to discover I could live without it. I spent most of the next 12 months working in my garden at home in Cheshire. Perhaps it was asking too much for a stress-free existence and it was anything but that. It seems there can never be a dull moment in the Souness household and there were more body blows to come. The month before I left Liverpool my father died. Then, my two German Shepherd dogs were shot by a farmer and my next-door neighbour was burgled and left bound and gagged by the intruders. In the space of a couple of weeks I was divorced and married Karen. We went to Las Vegas for the ceremony – that was the highlight of my year out of football. I had switched off completely from the game and did not miss it. I never went to a match, I never made contact with any of old my friends in the game and I could not even be bothered to watch matches on television.

It was ironic really. Karen was not a football fan when we met but because of my involvement she did become interested and regularly came to Anfield to watch games. Now the roles were reversed. I would be working away in the garden and she would call me to say there was a live game on the box. My response was, 'So what?' It did not mean anything to me any more. Once I did get back into the swing of things I was glued to the screen whenever football was shown and eventually she would start to complain. 'Can we watch something else for a change?' would be her plea. But for the best part of a year there was only one football fan in our house and it was not me.

We did fit in a holiday in Australia and I was tempted to a buy a place out there. The climate appealed to me and the pace of life was slower. Colin Irwin, a former Liverpool player, had settled in Perth and I spent some time with him and it was obvious he was very happy in Western Australia. We also went to Sydney and had dinner one night with Michael Parkinson and his wife. In those days he was spending up to three months of every year in Oz and the arrangement seemed to suit him. He was covering the Ashes Test series and had become a fan of the country. Hardly surprising. A combination of the outdoor life, good food and wine and a climate you could rely on was quite an attraction. No wonder the place has become so popular with British holidaymakers. It may be on the other side of the world but the journey is worth it. I had first visited Australia 20-odd years before and have been back on several occasions since then. I noticed a big change in the way the native Aussies lived their lives. In the early days the social scene revolved around the pub but that had all changed. They had woken up to the fact that they had a Mediterranean climate and could spend most of their time in the fresh air. That is what appealed to me because I have always been an outdoors person.

But most of my time that year was spent in my wellington boots with a spade in my hand or mowing the lawns. I would be out there straight after breakfast and if the weather held I would stay there pottering away all day. A sandwich at lunchtime was the only break I needed and the days seemed to fly by. I became totally engrossed in what I was doing and in the evening I would be planning what my tasks would be the following day. I did not need anything else to occupy my mind and that is a sure sign that you are happy in your work. There was plenty to do too. My back garden ended on the edge of a lake, and I had all sorts of weird and wonderful ideas about how to improve my property. Much of it involved physical work so I remained active while I was recharging the mental batteries.

It was excellent therapy for me. I am told some people go fishing to switch off from the cares and worries they have to handle when they are at work. Golf is another option. My garden became my escape route. I had not fallen out with football but I had found something else which proved to be more than a substitute. My new interest allowed me more time to think and I recalled the Liverpool years and analysed them. Spending all my time with Karen instead of rushing around the country also had an effect. She tells me that the year out changed me as a person. She says I started to listen more carefully to other people's points of view. I felt calmer and Karen played a big role in the change. When you have a partner you can confide in it does make a big difference. I began to realise what the old saying of a problem shared is a problem halved really meant. When my first marriage was going wrong I felt I was on my own but now I had a partner who was always willing to listen and offer support. I was quite content to be a housebound husband – something I could never imagine when I was giving my impression of 'Raging Bull' on the football pitch or as a high-profile manager. So I knew I had changed and hopefully for the better. The way I looked at it you had to be pretty stupid if you were incapable of learning from your mistakes.

My lifestyle had changed and so had the priorities. I was no longer a restless spirit. I could spend days at a time without going through the gates of my home. The garden fulfilled all my needs.

The loss of my father affected me badly and there were other traumas to come. When my neighbours were burgled, the police found them tied up and told me the villains had been carrying meat hooks in case they disturbed dogs. I immediately suspected they might have been targeting my house and were coming prepared to deal with my two German Shepherds. They were only a few months old and had replaced the two I lost. That was a sad episode. I have always been a dog-lover but apparently somebody had left a gate open and my pair had got into a field and killed a sheep. I had the task of bringing them home and burying them in the garden. It was not all sweetness and light during my self-imposed exile but overall it was beneficial and when the call came with the offer of a soccer job in Turkey, I was ready to seriously consider it.

16

Turkish Delight

Howard Wilkinson, the former Leeds and Sheffield Wednesday manager, was instrumental in my return to football. He had been offered the job at Galatasaray, one of the biggest clubs in Turkey. Howard, now the FA's Technical Director, turned it down and recommended me.

I had never been to Turkey but I took a call from one of the club's representatives and agreed to meet them in Paris. There are occasions when you know instinctively if something feels right and that was the impression I got when I met the people from Galatasaray. The guy who rang me initially became a great friend. His name was Denny Caouki and although he was not directly connected to the club, his brother was on the board. He attended the meeting in Paris along with the club president, the football director and the general manager. Very quickly I knew these were people I could work with and the job appealed to me. I remembered how well Galatasaray had performed against Manchester United in the European Cup and I knew Turkey was a football-mad country. When we arrived in Istanbul Denny was a constant support. He went out of his way to make us feel at home and if we ever needed any help on any matter we knew we could always rely on him. He was one of those guys who always had a smile on his face. You would think he did not have a care in the world although I discovered later that was not the case. But whenever I needed him he was always there without fail. I struck up an instant rapport with the football director who really ran the show. I would be working with him on a day-to-day basis so it was important that we understood each other. He was a comparatively young man for such a senior position but that was to his advantage because he found it easy to relate to the players and they held him in high esteem. The whole thing seemed to gel right away and I felt very upbeat about the job from day one.

Istanbul is a fascinating place and it was a totally new experience for Karen and me. We treated it as an adventure and loved every minute of it. I had signed a one-year contract and what happened after that was out of my hands. At most European clubs the board takes charge for a three-year period and then faces re-election. If they are removed all the people they have employed go with them. They had explained this to me when I met them in Paris. This was to be their final season before seeking re-election but if they survived they wanted me to stay on. So, later on, I was angry when it was reported I had been sacked after one year. What happened was my backers lost the election, a new board was installed and they naturally wanted to bring in their own people on the coaching side. It had all been explained to me in advance. If my people had won I would gladly have continued because by then I was enjoying the job and the lifestyle in Turkey.

We enjoyed a successful season on the pitch. Fenerbahce were the big city rivals and they were the club with the money. Galatasaray were trying to keep up with them and my task was to produce a team which would compete on level terms. We had two outstanding players – a midfield man, Tugay, and a striker, Hakan. When I arrived Hakan had been sold to Torino but he never settled in Italy and was back after three months. Both players were talented but their form suffered because of domestic problems. When Hakan rejoined the club he got married and then split with his wife after only three months, so his life was in turmoil. Tugay's form was also paying the price for trouble at home. These were the club's star players but it took them time to recover from their problems off the pitch and I needed to recruit some new faces if we were to give Fenerbahce something to worry about.

I brought in Barry Venison, Dean Saunders and Mike Marsh from England. Barry had fallen out with Kevin Keegan at Newcastle and I remembered Mike from my Liverpool days when he was a promising midfield player. He had moved on to West Ham and Coventry before I persuaded him to come to Turkey. I bought Dean from Aston Villa. I wanted Barry to play a holding role in front of the defence and he was very comfortable in that position. I think he found Turkey something of a culture shock and although I was happy with his performances on the pitch I have to admit the move did not really work out for him. When Southampton came in with an offer the club accepted it and Barry was happy to be going back to England.

Mike Marsh's wife had just had a baby and they did not find it easy adjusting to life so far from home. Eventually he moved back and signed for Ronnie Whelan who was managing Southend.

But they were all in my team when they first arrived, and Dean remained for the full season. I added another player with a Liverpool connection, Brad Friedel. He was playing for Brondby in Denmark but I soon realised I needed a goalkeeper and negotiated the deal with the American Football

Federation who held Brad's contract, and he was allowed to join us. A goalkeeper became a priority very early on. The three Istanbul clubs, Fenerbahce, Besiktas and Galatasaray play a pre-season Cup competition and my first-choice keeper was out with a damaged wrist. We lost 3–1 to Fenerbahce and then faced Besiktas in our stadium. I played the reserve, a guy called Mehmet, and he had a nightmare of a game. He conceded two bad goals and then started seriously headbutting the post! I had to take the poor fellow off and put the third choice on. That was when I turned to Phil and said, 'We sure need a new goalkeeper.' A Dutch defender, Ulrich Van Gobbel, completed my trio of foreign players – he came with me when I joined Southampton – and we had a terrific second half to the season. We did not lose any of the big games, finished fourth in the League and reached the Cup Final to face the old enemy, Fenerbahce.

That was a trophy I particularly wanted because of who was providing the opposition. When I first arrived at Galatasaray, a Fenerbahce official was reported as saying, 'What are they playing at employing a cripple as coach?' It was my intention to have a few words with that gentleman if the opportunity arose but the first time I saw him was in the Fenerbahce Stadium when we won the Cup. That should explain the way I reacted although a more restrained approach on my behalf might have been more sensible. The Cup Final was played over two legs and because both teams were based in Istanbul the interest in the city was enormous. The games were hyped to the hilt and it does not take very much for the Turks to get excited when you are talking about football. I thought I had played in the game's most passionate arenas in Liverpool, Glasgow and Italy but you can add Turkey to that list after what I witnessed in my year over there.

We won the home leg 1–0. In the return, Fenerbahce were 1–0 up after 90 minutes to take the tie into extra time. In the final minute the ball dropped invitingly for Dean Saunders and I just knew he was going to score. Dean is a really good striker of the ball and he lashed it in from 20 yards and we knew we had won the Cup. The celebrations started, our crowd was going crazy and our players went over to their end of the stadium to join them. Somebody produced a huge Galatasaray flag – it must have been ten by eight feet – and the players took it in turns to wave it. By then I was on the pitch and eventually the flag was handed to me. After I had held it for a couple of minutes I turned to pass it back to one of the players but by then they had all run to the halfway line. It was at that moment that I looked across into the main stand and spotted the character who had mocked me when I had first arrived. In that instant I thought, 'I will show you who is a cripple' and I carried the flag into the centre circle. I wanted to bury the pole as deeply as possible into the grass but when I first attempted to do so it nearly bounced out of my hands. They still use lime to mark the pitches in Turkey and this was like driving a pole into concrete. But I was determined to make my grand gesture and eventually planted it just off the centre circle. So there was the Galatasaray flag waving defiantly at the home of our biggest rivals.

I began to walk off the pitch but soon started to jog when I saw furious Fenerbahce fans trying to climb over the fences and get on to the pitch. That was when I thought discretion was the better part of valour and I wanted to reach the dressing room as fast as I could. The police were all lined up with their riot shields but I breathed a sigh of relief as I reached the tunnel. Suddenly I was whacked on the side of the head. A fan had somehow evaded the security net and was waiting for me. After smacking me once he stood back and a scuffle developed as I defended myself before the police intervened and sent me packing to the dressing room. I was in the clear because I had been attacked first and my only offence was to defend myself. The Fenerbahce fans went wild. They damaged our team coach as we left the stadium and, unbeknown to me, Galatasaray arranged for a couple of security guys to stand guard outside my apartment all night. Of course our fans loved every minute of it and the next day they were all wearing T-shirts depicting me planting the flag on the pitch. All around Istanbul I kept seeing these fans parading in their new shirts symbolising a famous victory for their club. It was a spectacular finale to a memorable year in Turkey.

We had begun the season with a series of friendly matches which quickly reminded me I had entered a totally different world. We played at Diyarbakir which is Kurdish country, close to the border with Syria and Iraq. When the plane landed there were military vehicles on the runway, Rambo-type guys all over the place with machine guns strapped to their shoulders, and a band to welcome us. It was quite a spectacle. The players were quickly surrounded by adoring fans who were excited at the prospect of one of the top teams coming to play in such an isolated area. Turkey is a huge country and just as Liverpool and Manchester United have a big fan base all over the UK, so the same applies with the big Turkish teams.

While the players signed autographs, Phil and I clambered on to our bus. We must have been waiting for half an hour before the players joined us and I feared the worst when I saw that Mike Marsh's and Dean Saunders's faces were covered in blood. I thought they had become involved in a fight until our hosts explained that it is a tradition in

Turkey to welcome visitors by sacrificing a sheep and daub-
ing them with warm blood. Everywhere we went in that area
the same thing happened. That year, I saw more sheep
slaughtered than a Welsh farmer. When we arrived at our
hotel they would produce another one and go through the
same routine before smearing blood over the coach's wind-
screen. It was a sign of respect and it was important that we
understood that. But it was a shock to the system. Before
one game I was just settling into my seat minutes before the
kick-off when I spotted another sheep on the halfway line.
Sure enough, before the game started, a man appeared with
a big, shiny knife and the same ritual was performed. I have
to say it never put me off kebabs but I did wonder what a
young boy in England would have made of it all. The youngsters in Turkey accepted it as part of a normal day and I am
not criticising the Turks. Their civilisation is as old as ours
so who is to say what is right and what is wrong? On that
same tour we stopped at a place called Van. It is famous for
its cats which have different-coloured eyes. When we drove
out of the airport I saw a sign which read, 'Turn left for the
city centre and right for Iran'!

The Turks love their football. They live and breathe the
game, even if the sheep don't. When people ask me about
Turkey I can only relate my experiences and it was one of
the best episodes of my football career. When you go abroad
on holiday the first question you usually get from friends is,
'What sort of a place was it?' I always approach it from a
different angle. My memories of different places are based
on the people and I got on famously with the Turks – with
the exception of the Fenerbahce faction, of course. I judge a
city or a country by the people I meet, not by the architec-
ture. On that score Istanbul is one of the most spectacular
cities in the world. We found the Turks warm-hearted and

welcoming. We made some very good friends over there and we have been back since to see them. Turkish delight? You bet.

17

Saints and Sinners

Lawrie McMenemy was the man who persuaded me to join Southampton. We had just returned from Turkey when he called and asked if I would be interested in taking over from Dave Merrington. I knew it was a nice part of the country and had heard stories of players who went to the South Coast and liked it so much they put down roots in the area once their careers had ended. I agreed to meet Lawrie and the Southampton chairman, Guy Askham, and they outlined how they saw the future of the club. As it turned out it never happened that way. The chairman painted a bright picture. Plans were well advanced to build a new stadium with a 30,000 capacity. That was essential because the Dell was too small for Premiership football. A 15,000 maximum was nowhere near enough and severely restricted their ability to keep pace with the big city clubs. The immediate priority was to remain in the top flight while they were still housed at the Dell, but there would be an opportunity to expand once they had moved into a bigger home.

Southampton is the only Premiership club in the South of England, with a huge catchment area, and they were confident we could double our attendances, which would give the club a vital financial boost and we could build from there. It sounded like an attractive proposition and I promised I would think about it and get back to them. The more I considered it the more it appealed and in the end I said yes and signed a three-year contract believing all their plans would come to fruition during that period. It was important that Lawrie played an active role and I wanted him to be working with me, otherwise I would have thought twice about taking the job. He has been in the game for such a long time and for many years he was 'Mr Southampton'. He knew the place inside out and his experience would be invaluable. He assured me he would be fully involved and I approached the task believing we could build a bigger and better Southampton. It was a different type of job from managing Liverpool or Rangers. There, success was always the requirement but at Southampton we would be looking to slowly turn the club into a major force. It was not going to happen overnight but in the long term there was an opportunity to establish a thriving club.

I made a deliberate decision to recruit younger players. The policy in the past had been to sign older people who were approaching the end of their careers. Southampton would get a couple of years out of them and then replace them with more of the same. That was not my idea of a long-term strategy. Southampton had been built on sand and lived from day to day. Somehow they had survived but there had been too many close calls with relegation, and I believed it was only a matter of time before they would pay the penalty and drop out of the Premiership. And any manager of any First Division club will tell you how difficult it is to get back once that happens. Southampton had another reminder of how precarious their position is when they just managed to stay up on the last day of the 1998–99 season.

I was looking to build a young side which would stay

together for five years and develop. Eyal Berkovic, Maik Taylor, Egil Ostenstad and Claus Lundekvam were unknown in this country when I signed them but they all made a significant contribution. They were the young, hungry types I was seeking and they quickly established themselves in the Premier League. I was under no illusions that the first season would be a test. It was a new team and foreign players need time to adjust to the pace and demands of English football but I was encouraged by their attitude and determination to succeed. Although we did drop dangerously close to the bottom of the table on occasions, I was confident we would stay up and that would provide the breathing space we needed. The highlight was a 6–3 win against Manchester United with Berkovic and Ostenstad sharing four of the goals.

Off the pitch I was growing concerned about certain events and I know Lawrie shared my misgivings. The board announced they were going to get involved with a retirement company and the whole structure of the club was going to change. Suddenly people were coming in who had no experience of football. It was an opportunity for a property deal and it certainly was not the future I had been sold when I was offered the job as manager.

We are talking about Southampton here. Their great strength over the years was their image as a family club and it had helped them through several crises. When the going got tough the fans rallied round and there was a bonding between them and the players which certainly helped to stave off the relegation threat on several occasions. Now that was all about to change and the supporters were quick to voice their disapproval. The news caused a storm though the town and hostility against the takeover began to mount. Public protest meetings were held, the media got involved and there were investigative TV programmes on the subject as they attempted to unravel the details of the proposed takeover.

New faces were appearing in the directors' box and some of the comments I overheard left me fearing the worst for the future of the club. Believe it or not, but on one occasion I could hear some unfamiliar voices demonstrating their complete ignorance about the game. It was a conversation which confirmed all my earlier concerns that we were about to embark down a rocky road which could undo all the good work Lawrie and I had started. I could scarcely believe my own ears when this plummy voice asked, 'Who are those chaps running up and down the touchline?' It was quietly explained to the poor soul that teams were allowed substitutes and they did warm-up exercises at the side of the pitch.

Perhaps it was no surprise that I got off on the wrong foot with Rupert Lowe who was destined to become the new chairman. Before he was appointed he started appearing at the training ground and the nature of his questions did not bode well for our future relationship. Directors should stay well away from the players' workplace but this was a new regime who either were not aware of how a football club is run or were determined to implement their own ideas. At that stage I decided to grit my teeth and just get on with it. My priority was keeping Southampton in the Premiership and I was prepared to leave any discussions about my future until the end of the season.

But any manager's patience would be sorely tried when he is asked, 'Are you sure the players are fit enough?' Then having it compounded by adding, 'I have a friend at Loughborough College who can help you.' I didn't need to be asked if Matt Le Tissier was the right man to captain the team. I required no advice on players' diets and I was not seeking to take a sports psychologist on board. These were just some of issues which cropped up as the new regime began to exert their authority.

In those days I was on a collision course with Rupert Lowe and it was all so unnecessary. In fairness to the man he has a much better grasp of what is involved after his two years in charge, but the mistakes of the early days could have been avoided with a more tactful approach. I accept he was new to football and he is not the first businessman to come into the sport and discover it bears no relation to anything else, but he did miss out on some excellent opportunities when he was trying to learn the ropes. He should have listened and learned from Lawrie McMenemy who could have taught him everything there was to know about Southampton FC. Lawrie knew the place inside out. He is a well-respected figure in the town and I am convinced with the aid of his contacts in the area the club would have received a more sympathetic hearing when they originally submitted their plans for a new stadium.

Alas, Mr Lowe thought he could combine the work of the retiring chairman, Guy Askham, plus the considerable duties which were Lawrie's domain. I can understand a new man wanting to become fully involved as soon as possible but while he was serving his apprenticeship he would have been better advised to listen to the experience Lawrie had to offer. I am sure that Mr Lowe, upon reflection, would agree that was the road he should have gone down when he first came into the club – it certainly would have avoided some of the problems which occurred. There were some lighter moments, however. He arranged for the squad to have a day out at a clay pigeon shoot in Berkshire. It provided a welcome change in routine and everyone enjoyed the day, including me. The trip coincided with a decent run of results for the team and the word from the boardroom was the management could thank the board for our change of fortune!

The situation was bad enough for me but imagine what was going through Lawrie's mind after all his time in the game. At the end of the season we went to Norway to watch a player and we were due to meet the chairman when we returned, to hear his plans for the following season. My mind was made up at this point and I knew if he did not come up with the right answers I would be leaving. The meeting did not go well. Mr Lowe proposed that Lawrie and I target potential new signings and he would negotiate the contracts with the players and their agents. I had been dealing with this aspect of the job for ten years but it was even worse for Lawrie. He had been in management for the best part of 30 years and was one of the most experienced men in the game. It was downhill all the way after that. Mr Lowe announced there would be a £2 million budget to strengthen the squad. I asked him if he realised that would buy next to nothing in the Premiership at a time when transfer fees were going through the roof. The situation was beginning to look hopeless. In many respects I felt sad about that. Lawrie and I were attempting to build a team for the future. We were both happy working at Southampton and could envisage some good times ahead for the club. Instead I resigned and Lawrie also left.

It is laughable for any Premiership club to set the spending budget at £2 million, especially when they were quick to enter the real world as sellers. I signed Kevin Davies from Chesterfield for £700,000 and Southampton sold him a year later to Blackburn for £7 million. Ostenstad cost £900,000 from Stavanger and now he is valued at around £6 million. I never saw Davies play in a Southampton shirt. I welcomed him to the club but I had left before the new season commenced. Perhaps even Mr Lowe was grateful for that business transaction – you don't often show that kind of profit on a player in just 12 months.

I remember the Davies signing for a different reason. Phil Boersma and I went to watch him on a freezing cold night in Chesterfield. George Graham and Danny Wilson were also present and although I thought he looked a decent prospect there was something else on my mind as we drove home. Never mind the player, I realised I had reached a watershed in my life. In the first half I had sat on the end seat of a row and the wind was howling straight into my face. For the second half I made sure I grabbed Phil's seat and he bore the brunt of it. But that was when I made the decision to buy a hat for the first time in my life. A bitterly cold night in Derbyshire had reminded me I was beginning to get a bit thin on top and it was time to do something about it! I also bought the player. Lawrie was on friendly terms with the Chesterfield chairman and we offered £500,000 on the strength of watching him just once. Chesterfield were on a great FA Cup run at the time and were reluctant to sell until that was over. In fact they were unlucky not to go all the way, when they had a goal disallowed in the semi-final against Middlesbrough. But for that they would have been at Wembley. I am sure young Kevin remembers those days for that reason – but me? I was more concerned about my receding hairline.

Southampton missed out on some other bargains. I signed Eyal Berkovic from Israel. The deal was we would pay £200,000 to have him on a 12-month loan and if we wanted to make the transfer permanent it would cost another £1 million. Unfortunately, the club lost out on a player who was subsequently valued at £5 million. They agreed to a clause that Berkovic's agent had included which gave the player the right to leave if he was not happy after the first season. When I resigned, Berkovic decided he was not staying either so Southampton had no option but to release him. He is now at my old Scottish rivals, Celtic.

The one that got away was Tore Andre Flo. When Ostenstad came over to train with us for a few days, he was joined by Flo who was playing for Bergen in Norway. Both players made an immediate impression and I was ready to buy the pair of them. Flo was just as keen as Ostenstad to join Southampton and this was long before Everton or Chelsea came on to the scene. Nobody in England was aware of Flo at that time. We offered the same price for Flo as for Ostenstad but Bergen held out for more, claiming he was the better player. Eventually we agreed a £1.5 million fee and I thought we had Flo in the bag. But the whole business had dragged on for so long Flo was persuaded to sit tight. His contract was coming to an end and his brother Jostein, who had played for Sheffield United, advised him to wait and see if any other clubs expressed an interest. Eventually he signed for Chelsea and is now one of the best strikers in the Premiership, attracting attention from other top European clubs.

I tendered my resignation while I was on holiday in Israel. It had been another eventful year but it could have been so much better. In many respects I had enjoyed it. I suspect Southampton will live to regret Lawrie's departure more than mine. He is now in charge of the Northern Ireland national side, but Southampton could ill afford to lose a man of such vast experience. He understood better than most how the club worked. Perhaps a correction is required here. It was no longer the place he once knew, so I don't think he shed too many tears when he walked out.

I went back to the Dell on two occasions in the 1998–99

season and observed the change in Rupert Lowe. I had a seat in the directors' box so I was able to watch him from close range and I have to say he has changed. He is not the first – nor will he be the last – businessman to discover that the world of football bears little relation to any other industry. There is no apprenticeship to prepare you for the day-to-day problems which arise at a football club. I spoke to him after the Saints had beaten Everton on the final day of the season to preserve their Premiership status and his relief and satisfaction was plain to see. He was on edge throughout the game, which was the clearest indication possible that he now fully understood what was at stake for Southampton. He has become a passionate football man. It may have taken two years to happen but it is good news for Southampton and the people he employs. I was very critical of him during my time as manager and I make no apology for that. I believe everything I said about him during my stay at the Dell was justified but that does not prevent me from wishing him well for the future.

18

Liverpool Revisited

Since leaving Anfield I have been back on only five occasions. Two were private visits to attend funerals but the other three were very public. My most recent visit was in September 1999 when I was working for Sky at the game against Manchester United. As manager of Southampton I was duty-bound to be at Anfield for our game and always had every intention of being there. The same applied when we played at Everton. The Liverpool match was just another game to me although I did wonder what sort of reception I would receive. That was more out of curiosity than anything else. I can honestly say I did not circle the date in the calendar or attach any greater importance to playing Liverpool than any other side. The team spent the Friday night a hotel at Haydock Park and when the coach drove through the Bill Shankly gates at the stadium my only real thought was how much things had changed since I was last at the ground.

As we disembarked I recognised many familiar faces and I must say the stewards and staff at Anfield were very friendly. You always get a few smart alec remarks from small groups of supporters at any football ground but nothing out of the ordinary happened when I walked through the door at Anfield. It was business as usual for me – the only difference was this time I was sat in a different dugout.

I remember Neil Ruddock and Jamie Redknapp were Liverpool substitutes on the day and they were seated close by. With Razor you can always expect a bit of a wind-up at some stage but it was good-natured stuff, while the crowd was more interested in Liverpool's performance than the fact that I was back in the stadium. I admit a good result would have given me immense satisfaction and it looked as though we would get it before Liverpool grabbed a late winner. That was the most disappointing aspect of the entire afternoon.

After the match I went for a drink and again it was all very civil. Kenny Dalglish and Sammy Lee joined me before David Moores put in an appearance. It was the first time I had spoken to him since I had left. It was all very polite and we chatted amicably for a few moments. Overall the entire visit had gone off without a hitch – apart from the result, which left me and Southampton feeling sorry for ourselves. As for Goodison – we lost that one too.

For every Michael Owen that comes along there are literally hundreds of young hopefuls who fall by the wayside. They are soon forgotten but there is one Liverpool teenager I shall never forget. Ian Frodsham was rated a genuine prospect before he was cruelly struck down. I have nothing but admiration for the manner in which his family dealt with a devastating personal tragedy. The first time we knew Ian might have a problem came when Steve Heighway took him to Florida on a summer soccer course. He complained that his back was hurting after the journey and the problem had not gone away when he reported back for pre-season training at Liverpool. He found it difficult to sit in one position for any length of time so we sent him for a medical examination. The results produced shattering news. Ian was suffering from a very serious form of cancer. We arranged to take him to a Birmingham hospital which specialised in treating Ian's condition. I had a big car so we used that, with Sammy Lee on board to make Ian as comfortable as possible for the journey. The specialist explained to Ian there was something they could do to help him but it was a life-threatening procedure. All the boy wanted to know was would he be able to play football again and the answer was an emphatic no. The treatment required would cause damage to his muscles and his career was over. That night in Birmingham he was told what the options were and they all involved major surgery.

I cannot begin to imagine what must have gone through his mind when he heard that news. His heart was set on becoming a professional footballer and although you can never say with certainty that a player of his age would make the grade, this was a lad with an inner strength and a steely determination which told me he would have gone on to become a very good footballer. Instead, with the support of his wonderful family, he fought it for as long as he could. He had a sister confined to a wheelchair and I could only admire the way his parents handled such savage blows to their children. I know they were very proud of Ian for the way he faced up to the inevitable. By the time Ian died I had left the club but what happened to him put my operation into perspective. How could I feel sorry for myself when I remembered Ian and the personal anguish of his family? My condition was curable and I was a grown man who had enjoyed some great times. Ian was just 17 and his whole life was ahead of him. To be struck down like that seemed so cruel and such a waste. I went to his home in Kirkby before the funeral and I remember the Liverpool club doctor who was also there remarking that he felt Ian looked so peaceful. I found it difficult to follow that train of thought but it is wonderful if you have that belief, and goodness knows Ian deserved to be at peace after what he had gone through. The family displayed incredible strength coping with this tragedy, particularly Ian's mother. What can be worse than losing one of your children? From the house we went to the church and then the graveyard. The club had arranged for everyone to go back to Anfield after the burial and although Ian's parents wanted me to join them I declined. I was determined to attend the funeral to pay my respects but I did not want to go to Anfield.

Bob Paisley died when I was working in Turkey but this was another funeral I felt it was my duty to attend. The church was packed and there were hundreds of Liverpool fans outside wanting to pay their respects to the most successful manager in the history of the game. I knew many players, past and present, would be there plus all the hierarchy from Anfield but I did not sit with them. They were all together in the centre section of the church and I was in a different area. I deliberately arrived early with Bob Rawcliffe, the man who owned the garage where Bob and I met before training and we left as soon as the service ended. A reception had been arranged at Anfield but once again I did not want to go. I was there to say goodbye to a man I had always respected and being able to make it to the church was all that mattered to me.

My abiding memory of Bob is from the night we won the European Cup in Paris. If you could choose one city in the world for a celebration, the odds are it would be Paris, and the vast majority of the Liverpool contingent did just that after we had beaten Real Madrid to win the trophy for the third time. But once the game was over the last thing on Bob's mind was a night on the town. Alan Hansen and I also remained in the hotel because our wives were not with us –

they were both expecting babies and had remained on Merseyside.

Eventually Alan and I ended up in Bob's room. There he was dressed in his cardigan and holding a glass of whisky in his hands. He was also wearing his trademark pair of slippers – something he did whenever possible because he suffered with ankle trouble and was always relieved when he could take his shoes off.

I thought to myself if only all those top coaches and managers could see Bob right now they would not believe their eyes. The uncrowned king of European football relaxing with his favourite tipple. He was not interested in seeking the limelight or milking the occasion. He was more interested in the fate of the horses he had backed that day and what was happening in *Coronation Street*! I am told that the first time Liverpool won the European Cup in Rome, Bob claimed he did not have a drink all night because he wanted to remember every single detail of the match and the celebrations which followed. When you have won it for a third time perhaps you are entitled to open a bottle! Even today it takes some believing – three European Cups for one manager.

He was unique. He believed football was a simple game and all about good players working hard for each other. As I noticed in that Paris hotel room, nothing fazed him. He was never big on coaching. You never saw him on the training ground with a clipboard, stopwatch and a whistle. He never concentrated on set plays and patterns. It was all about common sense with Bob. 'What is a blindside run?' he would ask, scoffing at the new jargon which was creeping into the game. He was dismissive of coaches who were experimenting with different playing formations. He firmly believed the old ways were the best, and who dared argue with a man who won so many trophies? The real key to his success was his gift of being able to judge a player and how he would fit into the scheme of things at Liverpool. That was what he really excelled at. And if he felt somebody was not right for the team he was quick to move them on. Appearances can be deceptive: Bob came across as everyone's favourite uncle but when it was necessary he could be ruthless. He liked a joke and he knew the players took the mickey out of him behind his back but he tolerated that as long as the team was winning. We did not kid ourselves: he knew everything that was going on at Liverpool.

Joe Fagan, who succeeded Bob, was more of an extrovert but was also a dedicated pupil of the Bill Shankly school of football. So was Ronnie Moran and all three were very similar in their approach to the game. None of them was interested in players who wanted to show how good they were as individuals. The only time you were encouraged to do something fancy on the ball was when you were pushed into a corner and there was no other way out apart from kicking it into touch. It had to be the final option when it was simply not possible to play it any other way. At Liverpool it was all about getting the ball forward quickly and accurately to the strikers and you were not encouraged to try and express yourself on the ball unless all other options were off.

While Bob was mild-mannered even when he was angry, Joe could fly off the handle and give you both barrels. He was more of a traditional coach than Bob. One day at training he was trying to get a message across to Alan Kennedy. He purposely made sure there was a group of players involved because he did not want it to appear as though he was picking on Alan for specific criticism. That was a smart move but when Joe got the impression Alan was only half-interested in what he was saying he really let rip. 'I have got better things to do if you are going to stand there wasting my time. All this is for your benefit and you are not listening to me.' Joe was clever. He would make his point and then invite players to give their opinion. He wanted us to feel as though we had an input and he was not laying down the law, when really he was just getting us to agree with what he wanted without giving the impression he was dictating the tactics.

I was on the receiving end of his temper on the way to a game at Southampton. We stopped at Oxford for lunch and there was an urgent message for me at the hotel to ring my brother's home in Edinburgh. My mother was gravely ill and he was warning me she might not survive the night. While I was talking to him the rest of the players had boarded the bus and I was delaying the party. Joe was a stickler for punctuality and when I eventually climbed aboard he really roasted me. I apologised and moved down the aisle to my seat and a few minutes later he joined me. Obviously he knew nothing about the reason I had kept everyone waiting but somebody must have told him about what was happening in Edinburgh, because he came and sat down beside me and chatted for a good 20 minutes. That was Joe. Hard but fair, and somebody you could always go to whenever you needed advice. I always classed Joe as a man's man. He will know that is intended as a compliment. My mother died that night when we arrived in Southampton.

Ronnie Moran came from a similar footballing background: honest, loyal and totally dedicated to the Liverpool cause. He was a good coach and I enjoyed my training when I was a player working with him. I don't suppose any other club will ever have the good fortune to have three men of their calibre working together for so many years. When people ask, 'What was the secret of Liverpool's success?' there were three characters in the old bootroom who could give you the answer.

19

The High Court

Winning battles on the football field became second nature to me when I was a player but I was in unknown territory when I entered the High Court in London in the summer of 1995 for a case which was to thrust me back into the headlines for all the wrong reasons. This was an issue more important than winning matches and I was determined to see it through to the bitter end whatever the consequences. It was a harrowing experience and one I would not like to repeat, but there comes a time in everyone's life when they have to stand up and be counted.

It all began one Saturday evening when I was pottering away in my garden and a reporter from the *News of the World* arrived at the gate to inform me my estranged wife had a highly critical article appearing in the *People* newspaper the next day, accusing me of all manner of misdemeanours. I declined to comment but at least I had been warned what to expect in the morning. I rarely buy newspapers, but on Sunday I drove into Knutsford to get a copy of the *People*. The shop was busy and I suppose a few customers recognised me because Knutsford is not a big town and it was no secret that I lived just down the road.

Imagine how I felt when I saw 'You Dirty Rat Souness' plastered across the front page. You immediately suspect everyone is staring at you and thinking, 'Is this guy really as bad as it says in the paper?' I felt embarrassed but I had no option. I needed to buy the newspaper and I picked one up and shuffled towards the assistant behind the counter trying to shield the offending headline in the misguided belief she would not take any notice which newspaper I was buying. It is strange how you react in certain circumstances but I felt like a thief in the night and could not get out of the shop quickly enough. I wanted to be back home as soon as possible to read the ghastly details and share my anger with Karen.

I could not believe what I was reading. I knew I had to fight this slur – whatever it would take – and I was aware it would be a very expensive business if I lost. It crossed my mind that I might have to sell my house if it all went wrong just to pay the legal bills, but this was a matter of honour and there was no way I was going to allow the charges to go unchallenged. I immediately contacted my lawyer and informed him I wanted to sue for libel and I wanted the best barrister available. I knew what I was letting myself in for – an individual tackling a national newspaper – but I was prepared to take it all the way unless the *People* backed down and apologised. I was no stranger to publicity as a player and a manager but this was something entirely different. It does not matter who you are – when you are falsely accused of ill-treating your children there is only one course open to you. Come what would I was set on clearing my name.

I was being portrayed as some kind of evil Svengali-type figure who wanted to exercise total control over my ex-wife even though we had been living apart for two years. I would never do anything to harm or damage my children and I could not get the imprint of that shocking 'You Dirty Rat Souness' headline out of my mind.

George Carman QC had been employed by Mirror Group Newspapers and although I knew little about the legal system I was well aware that he was one of the most eminent men in his field and it did not help my peace of mind when somebody kindly informed me he had never lost a major case! The battle lines were being drawn and I was under no illusions about the ordeal which lay ahead. My lawyer made an appointment for me to meet Richard Rampton who was also one of the country's leading libel barristers and we immediately hit it off. He read through the papers and told me, 'You will win this and they will settle with you.' That was an enormous encouragement and instantly removed any misgivings I might have had about taking this all the way.

I was very comfortable dealing with Richard Rampton but fate suddenly intervened and he was no longer able to represent me. He apologised profusely but a bigger case had cropped up which would occupy all his time for an indefinite period. He had been engaged by McDonald's, the fast-food chain, to contest a claim that their food was bad for your health. A former postman and a former gardener had distributed a leaflet, *What's Wrong With McDonald's*, and the company sued them. Richard jokingly said to me he would retire when that case ended but it was going to occupy all his time. In the event it became the longest libel trial in English history, lasting 314 days and costing an estimated £10 million. I was back to square one and looking for somebody else to represent me. It was a blow because Richard Rampton struck me as the ideal man to fight my case. When I eventually got to the High Court, the McDonald's case was also being heard in the same building and I often bumped into

Richard. He was obviously following events in my case and was always ready with some encouraging words.

Fortunately he came up with the name of Lord Williams and within ten minutes of meeting him I knew I would be able to work with him too. It is vital you feel confident about the person who is going to court on your behalf. When you are signing cheques for £30,000 every other month and you are funding something which could cost you £700,000 if you come unstuck you are playing for massive stakes. My resolve was even stronger at this point and I was ready to fight to the bitter end.

I was in front of the media circus once again. The case lasted for two weeks and it was an incredible experience. A rollercoaster ride, according to the newspapers which lapped up everything that was said and gave the case maximum publicity. I accepted that as one of the pitfalls of having a reasonably high profile. According to the press, I had good days and bad days as various points were argued out in the full spotlight of the public gaze. It was explained to me that a libel case is basically all about finding as much dirt as you can to embarrass the other side. It may not have any relevance to why you are suing or being sued – it is all about blackening the name of the other party. The case began with the legal arguments which cannot be reported until a verdict has been reached. On the first day I remember Peter Robinson was in court because many of the events related to my time at Liverpool.

I was in the witness box for a day and a half. I had a sheaf of papers which I needed to study so I was prepared for any questions which were fired at me. Lord Williams opened the proceedings so I was able to give my side of the story. I was comfortable at that stage because he was representing me and this was a friendly exchange but when he sat down and

George Carman immediately went on the offensive I was taken by surprise because nobody had warned me that was how the system worked. My reaction was to fight back and I did not emerge very convincingly from that contest. I wanted to argue with Mr Carman. Later, I reflected on my performance and I realised that I had played into his hands.

The following day I had learned my lesson and handled myself correctly. It was pointed out to me that this case was all about the jury believing what I said and I would not be helping myself by encouraging a confrontation with the opposition. I think I won the case on the second day although you could never take anything for granted, and it was another week or more before it was all over. You can never be totally prepared for every question. I remember on the second day I was asked where I had gone for dinner the previous evening and who did I go with. I answered quite openly that I went to an Italian restaurant with my Scottish lawyer, Jim Keegan. 'You did not talk about the case of course?' was the question, and that was when I realised somebody had been following me to see who I was spending time with. That was a shock because I did not realise such things could happen, but I was learning fast.

Two nights before the case was due to end my lawyers received a call offering an out-of-court settlement. I agreed and my team hammered out an acceptable figure only for the defendants to change their mind. It did, however, seem to be a good sign if they were having doubts at this stage. We had no option but to wait for everything to take its course. The best way to describe it is as extremely exciting because you are living on the edge as you wait for the climax of the proceedings. On the final day the judge, Mr Justice Morland, delivered his summing-up speech. To me it all sounded so positive and I felt elated by the tone and content of what he had to say.

The last thing I wanted to do was to interrupt him but I had no choice. I was taking tablets to ensure my kidneys functioned properly and that necessitated regular visits to the toilet. Imagine my embarrassment when my legal team was forced to request a short adjournment while I left the courtroom.

The judge described how much I loved my children and how generous I had been in providing a home for them and my estranged wife. The only jarring note was a reference to the fact that I had failed to see my children before my heart operation. It was too late by then to inform him that my wife had refused them permission to come to the hospital. Karen had begged her to allow them to visit, in case it was the last time they would see me, but she was adamant they would not be coming. Overall I felt happy that he had believed my version of events and I was feeling confident when he had finished his speech.

When the jury went out to deliberate, Karen and I went for a walk in a park at the back of the High Court. There were a few winos around and one little incident helped to ease the tension. One of them recognised me and called out, 'Hey, are you Souness?' I replied, 'Yes' and he followed up with, 'Is that your daughter with you?' At least that produced a smile from Karen. Shortly afterwards we were told the jury had reached a verdict, even though it seemed no time at all since they had left the court. It was two hours in fact, and my lawyers considered that to be a good sign.

The judge asked the foreman to stand up and asked him, 'How do you find, for the plaintiff or the defendant?' When we realised we had won I cannot describe the feeling of relief that flooded over me. Suddenly all the worry and mental stress which had burdened me for three years slipped from my shoulders. Karen burst into tears and I just slumped in my seat – grateful that it was all over.

I was awarded £750,000 plus costs – the third biggest libel award ever in England. But it was not about money. It was all about winning and clearing my name. Mirror Group Newspapers announced they would appeal and £500,000 was immediately frozen. In the end I received £250,000 but the money was irrelevant. My reputation had been vindicated and that was all I wanted. I felt very bitter towards my first wife because she knew the accusations were untrue and it was so unnecessary to drag such a sordid story through the courts.

I would not want to go through another experience like that, but it was something I had to do and if a similar occasions arose ever again I would be prepared to fully pursue the matter, whatever the risk and the cost.

20

The Italian Experience

My time at Torino is best described as a brief interlude, and that is putting it mildly. After resigning at Southampton I received a call from Italy asking if I would meet a couple of people who were coming to England. Originally they had been interested in signing Eyal Berkovic after buying Torino, once one of the giants of Serie A but now struggling in Serie B.

They told me they used to watch me when I played for Sampdoria and wanted me to join them to revive Torino. The idea appealed to me but as soon as I arrived in Turin for pre-season training I realised I had made a major mistake. I was not aware that a brand new squad of 17 players had been recruited just before I arrived. My new employers had taken the word of agents, journalists and friends to bring in the new faces and then said to me, 'Here is your squad, now let's get promotion.'

There was not a penny to spend but I did sign Tony Dorigo for nothing from Leeds under the Bosman Ruling and it quickly became evident that he was the best player I had. It was a doomed venture from the start and another example of people with stars in their eyes but no idea of the size of the task.

Torino are *the* club in Turin but their neighbours, Juventus, draw their support from all over the country. It is the same situation which applies in Manchester, where City have a big local following but United draw fans to Old Trafford from all over England, Ireland, Scotland and Wales.

Football is full of dreamers with their grand plans to achieve success but the bottom line is you need money to make it all come true and Torino were skint. Of course if they could reclaim their place in Serie A they could take off again, but many years of mismanagement had left them languishing in no man's land and it was soon obvious to me that was not about to change. Imagine the same situation in England: a club appoints a new manager and then says: 'By the way we have signed all the players you need. All we want you to do is mould them into a winning team and get us promoted. And don't bother trying to buy anyone else because we don't have any money.'

That was my situation, and I was there for just six games. We won two, lost two and drew the others but then the guys who had headhunted me said, 'We feel we need a coach with experience of Serie B.' I was not complaining because I already knew in my own mind that it was not going to work and I was happy to get out. Torino had been out of the top flight for a long time and I realised with the non-existent resources available to me that I would not be able to deliver the promotion they craved. Perhaps they have learned their lesson that the best coach in the world would have been unable to satisfy their dreams, unless he was given a realistic budget and the freedom to sign the players he wanted on board, because they did gain promotion at the end of the 1998–99 season. And I am pleased about that. It could be the springboard for the club to move forward and revive the glory days.

I walked into an impossible situation at Torino and vowed I would not make the same mistake again. Little did I know my next step would lead me into a much crazier situation at Benfica. Who ever said it was easy to live and learn?

21

The Benfica Nightmare

The Benfica episode ended in sadness and bitter recrimination. It could have been so different. When I look back at my time in Portugal it is with a combination of pride in a job well done and disappointment that it all finished on such a sour note. My dispute with the man who appointed me, club president Joao Vale e Azvedo, is now the subject of legal action and until the matter is resolved I am unable to give a complete account of the reasons behind my departure from Benfica.

I have no doubt at all that I did the best job of my managerial career during my 18 months at Benfica and I know nobody could have achieved more in the circumstances. Make a note of this prediction. If my successor, Jupp Heynckes, finds himself working under the same conditions I would put money on him walking out before Christmas.

The German will think he has left one of the great clubs in Europe – Real Madrid – to join another of equal standing but in my view Benfica's glory days are history and will remain so until the club is restructured from top to bottom. That will take money, willpower and enterprise.

Perhaps I should blame Steve Archibald, who made the decisive first call which eventually sent me to Portugal. Steve, a former Tottenham and Scotland striker, was working with FIFA agent Blair Morgan, and he approached me to see if I would be interested in a big European club which was in difficulties. This happened two weeks after my short stay at Torino had ended and I told him I had just left a big European club which was in difficulties and I did not want to go down the same road again. But I was intrigued to know the identity of the club involved and of course I was impressed when he told me it was Benfica.

I had played in their magnificent stadium for Liverpool and Scotland and remembered the passion of the fans and the atmosphere generated by an 80,000 crowd. Perhaps I should have done my homework there and then but Benfica boast such a famous name you automatically bracket them with Real Madrid, Barcelona, Bayern Munich and the top Italian clubs. Everyone remembers when the great Eusebio was a world-class star at Benfica. Next to Pele he was rated the best around and the most gifted player to have emerged from Africa. They were in their pomp in those days but time can play tricks with the memory. Benfica's last European Cup success was in 1962 and a lot of water has gone under the bridge since then. Even at domestic level, where they enjoy the same popularity as Manchester United in England, they have not won the Portuguese Championship for six years. That is now dominated by Porto, which is regarded as a provincial club by the inhabitants of Lisbon. My brief was firstly to restore Benfica as the country's top club and then plan a major assault on Europe. I presumed that funds would be made available to build a strong squad so Benfica could once again become a force to be reckoned with.

At this time Joao Vale e Azvedo, a prominent Lisbon lawyer was bidding to become the new club president. In Portugal they hold an election every three years for that post and my invitation to meet him came at the height of his campaign. Whoever wins appoints his own coach and can also recruit his own administrative staff. No wonder football becomes so chaotic at a club like Benfica. They are desperate for success but if the president fails to deliver during his term in office he is voted out and his staff – starting with the coach – go with him. A new president then begins the routine all over again with a different coach and backroom people. It is a version of musical chairs but it denies the club the one factor which is so important and that is stability.

Having said that, Portugal certainly has its attractions – especially when you are dining in a five-star restaurant overlooking the Atlantic and the sun is shining. In a nutshell, if he won the election he was offering me the role of coach and it was the start of a frantic week in which I was living out of a suitcase continually catching flights to and from Portugal.

This was the schedule: Tuesday, Heathrow. Fly to Lisbon to meet the president elect. Wednesday, return to UK after talks. Thursday, back to Lisbon. Friday, return to UK. Saturday, fly to Porto to watch Benfica play for the first time at Chaves on the Spanish border. Saturday evening, a seven-hour drive back to Lisbon to catch the early Sunday morning flight to Heathrow.

I agreed to accompany Mr Azvedo to a rally of Benfica supporters while he was on the campaign trail. That is how I found myself back in Lisbon 48 hours later, effectively in the role of his running mate. It was pure showbiz. I had been warned there would be 10,000 football supporters crammed into a huge hall to hear the words of the man who wanted to take charge. Everything was stage-managed so that the president elect did not make his grand entrance until the hall was full and he would appear as the top-of-the-bill attraction.

When we did appear a band struck up and there was bedlam. We were escorted on to a stage where Mr Azvedo addressed a wildly excited crowd and although I did not understand what he was saying he obviously struck a chord with his audience because wild bouts of cheering interrupted his speech which told me they liked what they were hearing. The next day I was back in Winchester when he telephoned to say he had been elected and I could start work straight away.

Benfica was lying seventh in the table on my first day as coach but a title bid had not been ruled out and, swept along by everyone's enthusiasm, I was optimistic that we could rapidly climb into a challenging position.

When I started my job I knew nothing about the problems which were about to surface. I could see this spectacular stadium, superb training facilities; I knew about the fanatical support the club could generate, and I was formulating my own plans.

An agent recommended Karel Poborsky to the president and he sounded me out for my opinion before deciding to proceed with the transfer which would cost £2 million. Poborsky had been a big success at Euro 96 before he was signed by Manchester United and I knew he was a crowd-pleaser. He was having problems obtaining a new work permit to remain in England and I knew his pacy style would appeal to Portuguese fans. I had every reason to believe the bandwagon was starting to roll with his arrival and I expected others to follow. It is history now but United had to fight long and hard to receive the transfer money.

That was an embarrassing situation for me. I know Alex Ferguson and I had met United's solicitor Maurice Watkins on several occasions. Alex understood how these problems could arise when a foreign club was involved but it did not do my reputation any good. It is only logical for people to think that I must have been aware of the delay in paying the fee when in fact I was completely in the dark. Alex did mention it to me when we bumped into each other but he was not on the warpath because he knows that a coach working in Europe does not have the same input as an English-based manager when dealing with transfers.

Despite that hiccup Benfica continued to give the impression that they were serious players in the transfer market. They sent Blair Morgan to Italy to offer $14 million for Rui Costa who was playing for Fiorentina. Costa, one of Portugal's favourite players, is a class act and naturally our supporters were excited at the prospect of him joining Benfica. I later discovered that buying Costa was a key element in the president's election manifesto. Another $12 million offer went to Anderlecht in an attempt to sign Par Zetterberg.

If you look at my record of buying and selling in the end I was in profit, but I was expected to produce a championship-winning team and when we qualified for the European Cup they seriously thought we could win that too. In England some First and Second Division clubs have a bigger budget than the one I had at Benfica. That is why I shall always argue I did a fantastic job and left with a clear conscience.

In the transfer business Benfica resembled a supermarket with an endless stream of activity. When people ask me why I allowed Emerson Thome to join Sheffield Wednesday on a free transfer I have to admit I knew nothing about it. Apparently he left while I was in charge but I would not know the guy if I fell over him. To the best of my knowledge I never met him and never saw him play. In my first season I was assessing the squad and quickly realised I had an outstanding defender in a Paraguayan named Gamarra. He was a great guy and excelled in the World Cup in France. He looked like a Scotsman, all red hair and freckles, and I knew he would be a key man in my plans. So what happened? He was sold by Benfica to a Brazilian club. That is how it works in Portugal. Later, I found he was back in Europe, signing for Atletico Madrid for £6 million for the 1999–2000 season.

The Portuguese players are technically highly gifted but they all want to be the star of the show. Give them the ball and they can look good. The only problem is they are reluctant to do the donkey work when the opposition has possession. Talented individuals, but they put themselves before the team which is why I lowered my sights in the transfer market and aimed to bring in some solid British stock to give the side some backbone. In my first season I knew we were some way short of being a good side but we kept winning matches and climbing the table. Brian Deane arrived from Sheffield United for £1.5 million although they also had to wait to be paid. I sold him a year later to Middlesbrough for £3 million. I snapped up Mark Pembridge from Sheffield Wednesday for nothing under the Bosman Ruling and Michael Thomas came from Liverpool on a free transfer. Scott Minto, from Charlton, was already at the club when I arrived, and in my second season I bought Gary Charles from Aston Villa, Steve Harkness from Liverpool and signed Dean Saunders on a free transfer from Sheffield United.

Once again I was a wheeler and dealer, looking for bargains while expected to build on our success of the first season when we finished runners-up to Porto and qualified for the Champions League. That was quite an achievement but I knew nothing less than the title in my second year – or winning the European Cup – would keep the wolf from the door. In Europe we narrowly failed to qualify for the knockout stages and ended third in the League. Not enough, especially as the president announced at the start of the season that we would win the championship. A coach needs that type of talk like a hole in the head. That is the way it is in Portugal. Too many people are living in the past and the coach is never more than a couple of games away from the sack. They want immediate success and with no disrespect to the players I brought in it was certainly asking too much of them to deliver prizes of that magnitude.

I sold Minto to West Ham for £1 million, Martin Pringle to Charlton for £800,000 and the remaining Brits were made available for transfer when I left. Benfica knew they could make money by selling them back to England. Pembridge, Charles and Harkness have all since joined English clubs for a combined total of £2.6 million, and Saunders is now at Bradford City. Some of my signings bore the brunt when results did not go our way and I put that down to the fans. They are very patriotic and I admire them for that but they allow themselves to be blinded when it comes to football. Their local favourites can do no wrong and will always be excused whereas any error by a foreign player is not forgotten. It would not have made any difference if my signings had come from Spain, Germany, Italy or South America – they would have received the same treatment. Michael Thomas in particular was given a rough ride. It is a strange situation. The Portuguese are pro-British – the history books show they are our oldest allies. It is a great place to go for a holiday and British visitors are treated with courtesy and respect but all that goes out of the window when football is the subject. The British lads were happy to play for Benfica but some of the players I inherited had been elevated to superstar status, when their ability hardly justified it. These were the same players who were drifting along in eighth place when I arrived. We did improve them with stricter training techniques and concentrated coaching sessions but you can only develop a player so far. If they lack the ability to become a better player there is nothing you can do about it: they need the inner desire to improve.

To give you an example of how Portuguese players think, there was an amusing little cameo towards the end of the 1998–99 season. Overall they are physically small and I wanted to improve their body strength. We bought some extra exercise machines and installed them in the gym to encourage the younger players to spend more time improving their fitness levels. The idea was met with indifference. The machines were ignored for several weeks and then suddenly there was frantic activity in the gym with players working on the bikes and weights. Foolishly I thought the penny had dropped and the players were responding. I asked one of the backroom staff why there had been this change of heart and the explanation left me bemused. 'Summer is on the way and they want to look their best for the girls when they go to the beach.' There was no answer to that.

Believe it or not, but over the course of a two-year period before I arrived, Benfica bought and sold a total of 100 players. Great business for agents and the players concerned but typical of the muddled thinking at the club. It was a recipe for disaster and symptomatic of what had been going on for a long time. No wonder they were in deep trouble. Benfica had been in turmoil since their golden era of the 1960s. You simply cannot buy a new team every year and expect it to click. It takes time – the one commodity you are denied in Portuguese football. Our great rivals Sporting Lisbon for example, went through four different coaches in my first season.

It could only happen over there but in one instance they actually signed a Brazilian, Paulo Nunes but only bought half of him! Imagine that situation in England. You buy 50 per cent of a player. An agent had bought out Nunes's contract from his previous club so in effect he owned him.

The way it worked was if we eventually sold the player for a profit the agent would claim 50 per cent of the money because he had an equal stake with Benfica. Mind-boggling. Nunes was one of five Brazilians on the books and I quickly realised they were not good enough and would have to be moved on. But how do you sell half of a player?

Football fans in Portugal have a totally different outlook on the game. Their idea of being a supporter bears little relation to the typical British fan who sticks by his team through thick and thin. The country has a population of 10 million, and 6 million claim to follow Benfica. I became tired of people coming up to me in the streets of Lisbon and proudly waving a card which identified them as a Benfica supporter. Yes, they are all members and pay a small annual subscription but I would never classify them as fans in the British tradition. Our gates proved that. We had nearly 80,000 one season when we played Boavista but because we lost the attendance dropped to 15,000 the next time we were at home.

Those who do turn up regularly come to criticise. You have got ten minutes to score a goal before they start whistling and booing. It is the philosophy of the bullfight when there must always be a victim: theatre rather than football. It is not about backing your team. They want instant entertainment and if it is not on offer they immediately turn. An individual will always be signalled out and there will be howls of rage if he makes the most minor of mistakes while others remain untouchable no matter how badly they are performing.

Working in so many different countries has made me appreciate the virtues of the typical British fan. As a nation we are far from perfect, but believe me you won't find a better environment when it comes to football. Loyalty is the key word for those guys who follow Liverpool, Rangers,

Manchester United and all the other big clubs. Even in Turkey where they get very excited about the game they stick with their team and the whistles and jeers only come at the end if the result is the wrong one.

I knew I was on borrowed time as early as December 1998 when we just failed to qualify for the knockout stages of the European Cup. We were never lower than third in our own league but there was a perceptible shift in the attitude of some of the club officials when we dropped out of Europe. I had seen those signs before so I knew it boiled down to a case of the championship or bust. I was disappointed to go out of Europe but I maintain that we exceeded all expectations by qualifying in the first place. A classic example of making a rod for your own back.

The Boavista defeat in April made it virtually impossible for us to win the title and more people started keeping their distance because they knew – as I did – that the writing was on the wall. It did not worry me. I knew what I had achieved and that nobody could have done better in the circumstances. In my own mind I knew I was a better manager than when I first started at Rangers. The next move was down to Benfica and it was not long coming after the Boavista defeat. My time was up, and my successor, Jupp Heynckes, turned up for the game against Porto while I was still in charge of the team.

I am sure he will be watching events with interest. Before he even starts he knows the requirement is to produce a successful team from day one. That requires funding and unless that is available it will be considered a disaster if the championship evades them again. I know from my experience that managing clubs like Rangers and Liverpool was a cakewalk compared to the problems which exist at Benfica. It can be a demanding life working in Britain but it pales into insignificance compared to management in Portugal. I took on mission impossible and very nearly pulled it off. At Benfica, football is expected to finance all the other activities associated with the club's name. Like so many other Continental clubs it embraces all manner of sports, including athletics, basketball, handball, swimming and cycling teams which all come under the Benfica umbrella.

The success they craved was an impossibility in the circumstances. Hand on heart I can say Alex Ferguson could not have done a better job. Thirty years in the game failed to prepare me for what I experienced. And it is such a pity. If they could put their house in order it could be a wonderful club. The facilities are in place, Lisbon is an attractive city and because of Portugal's links with Brazil they can attract players from South America as well as Europe.

Despite the way it ended, the plus side is I have learned more about myself, the game, and dealing with a certain type of person. All of which helps to broaden your horizons. You could say that my managerial experiences so far have produced a mixed bag but wherever I have gone I have always tried to view it as an adventure.

I have come away from Benfica bloodied but unbowed. Football continues to draw me like a bug and I shall take the plunge again when the right job comes along, but next time I shall do my homework properly. Working abroad has lost some of its appeal but you can never say never in this business. Karen wants us to stay in England with the new baby arriving and I have always said the family must come first.

There is always the garden if I need to wait for another opportunity. I have barely lived in my house at Winchester for the last three years because football took me abroad, so now, at the age of 46, perhaps the time has come for a change of direction. The game will always be part of me but I have shown I can live without it at certain stages and that has not

changed. I am an older, wiser football manager these days –
and a more mature person as a result of my experiences at
home and abroad.

22

My Pal Phil

Ask any manager what he wants from his staff and the first word would be trust, which brings me to Phil Boersma. I have known him for 25 years and wherever I go in football I want him to be there. We first met at Middlesbrough. I had joined the club from Tottenham when Phil arrived from Liverpool. We were two young boys sharing digs and we immediately hit it off. He was forever going on about Liverpool and what a great club it was and indirectly he played a part in my move to Anfield.

As a Liverpool player he had the misfortune to be around at the same time as Kevin Keegan and John Toshack, and although he scored plenty of goals he realised he was never going to convince Shankly to make him the first choice when they were available. That is how he ended up at Middlesbrough but he has always been a Liverpool fan and that will never change. I call him Peter Pan because he is now 50 years of age and yet remains in peak physical condition. He is fortunate that he can have a drink when he fancies it but never has a problem sweating it off in the gym the next day. He trains as hard today as when he was a player. It was Phil who first told me of Liverpool's interest in me. He was a big pal of Bob Rawcliffe, the man who owned the garage where Bob Paisley was to be found on most mornings. Phil was in a regular contact with that garage in West Derby and would pass on the latest messages that Liverpool were watching me on a regular basis and their interest was growing stronger. But it was in the North-East where our long friendship had its roots.

When I joined Liverpool we went our separate ways for a few years but always stayed in touch. I told him if I ever went into management I would want him to work with me and that is what happened at Rangers. Phil was at Doncaster Rovers when I placed the call and he needed no persuading to come to Glasgow.

He has been everywhere with me since, apart from Torino, and if I take another management job he will be the first person I will appoint. My only regret is that life was difficult for him when we returned to Liverpool. I felt bad about that because he did not deserve the treatment he received. Going back to Liverpool meant so much to him but there was obvious resentment in some quarters and he did not deserve that.

Maybe he was still pictured as the happy-go-lucky youngster he was when he played for Liverpool. Whatever the reason it was not easy for him and I was aware of that situation very quickly.

He was never allowed to do the job he did best at Liverpool but he did not make a big fuss about it although I knew he was unhappy about certain events that occurred. So was I. He was not a threat to any of the backroom staff at Liverpool but they did not exactly welcome him with open arms and that was tough on Phil. He loved the club as much as anyone and the prospect of going back after being away for so many years had him jumping for joy. He deserved better, and I was disappointed that he was made to feel like an outsider by some of the staff. The role he performed at Rangers and later at Southampton, Galatasaray and Benfica never applied at Liverpool. In the end I had to invent a title for him – rehabilitation officer – but it should never have been necessary for me to justify what he did. When Liverpool asked me to become manager I made it clear from the start that I was bringing Phil with me and they had no objection. The problems began when he started work and he did not deserve that. Every manager needs someone he can confide in and Phil has always been there for me since we were reunited at Rangers.

Contrary to all the rumours I did not change anything on the training ground at Liverpool. In fact one of my biggest mistakes was not doing something about it. Phil was unable to do his job and nothing was allowed to disturb the old routines which had become set in stone over the years. It is a myth that I went in and ordered a complete revision of the training methods. With hindsight I should have ordered more changes but Liverpool have always been reluctant to alter the programmes first established by Shankly all those years ago. They only knew one way and although it had served them well for decades they were slow to accept that the game has moved on.

The best way to describe Phil is as a latter-day Reuben Bennett. That name may not register with younger Liverpool fans but Reuben was part of Bill Shankly's bootroom with Bob Paisley, Joe Fagan and Ronnie Moran. Phil can do all the physical work demanded of the players and he can still keep up with them on training runs. He has his own opinions about the game and as he has got older he has not been afraid to express them. We do agree on most things – more or less – but he is not a yes man and it is healthy when we do disagree because he will say his piece when it feels it is necessary.

When he was a young player at Liverpool he was always game for a laugh and liked to enjoy himself. He has always been great company on a night out but the earlier image has stuck with him and that gives people the wrong impression. He is a much more serious person these days and can wear his grumpy hat on occasions. He takes the game seriously, can be outspoken, and anyone who thinks they know Phil because of the old days would be in for a shock if they sat down with him today to talk football.

There was one occasion at Rangers which he remembers for all the wrong reasons but it still gives me a chuckle. I arranged for Daley Thompson's coach, Frank Dick, to give the players a motivational talk before a Cup tie against St Johnstone. We had promised them a trip to Eilat in Israel if they won but when Frank started talking about mountain men and valley men Phil sensed the players were not really on the same wavelength.

Frank's point was they had to decide what they wanted to be – either high achievers or just content with their lot. I found his talk interesting but it did go on for a good 20 minutes and Phil sensed the players were switching off long before he had finished. When he reached the 'mountain men and valley men' bit, Phil was ready to crack up, and just to spoil a pleasant few days beside the Red Sea, we only drew the game and the trip to Israel was cancelled!

Phil is more than a mate – he is somebody I can trust completely and you cannot put a price on that. I know instinctively that I can bounce ideas off him and be sure of an honest answer even when he may totally disagree with the suggestion. A manager needs people prepared to argue the toss if they feel passionately about an issue, but all too often these days individuals are more concerned with protecting their jobs, and it is easy to just agree with every idea the boss proposes rather than stand your ground and express an honestly held opinion. Phil will do that because he knows I will listen. Managers need solid input from their staff but they don't always get it.

Wherever football takes me next you can be sure Phil will be at my side.

23

The PR Game

Dealing with the media on a day-to-day basis comes as second nature to some people in football but I admit it took me a long time to realise the importance of this aspect of the job. Certainly today it is essential to be able to cope with the demands of the press, radio and television because of the enormous interest the game now generates.

When I was a player I hardly gave it a second thought. I was in a winning team and that was all that seemed to matter. When I became manager of Rangers we were successful on the pitch and I unwisely believed that was the answer to everything. Perhaps I should have been taking notice of Ron Atkinson even then because he has perfected the art of keeping the media satisfied. It can be time-consuming but every game is so closely scrutinised these days I appreciate the need for managers to be available to put across their point of view.

I never tried to win friends in the media and although I would not say I am an expert, today I am certainly more aware of what is required. Some people in my industry have turned becoming a household name into an art-form even though in my opinion many of them don't deserve to be as famous as they are.

At Liverpool the players were never encouraged to court publicity. If your name appeared in the newspapers too often you were soon taken down a peg or two. Ronnie Moran or Joe Fagan would be quick to blame anyone who had an off-day for spending too much time talking to the press. That fashioned my attitude to the media and it took me a long time to soften my views. I thought I had a reasonable working relationship with the journalists I saw on a regular basis at the training ground or after matches, but we were all taught to be careful when we were interviewed. The same applied with Kenny Dalglish and he found it difficult to communicate once he became a manager.

And don't forget that we were a team winning all the major honours. That is why I can understand the current Liverpool squad being reluctant to say much. When you are not getting results it is inevitable you will be criticised, so the natural reaction is to not speak in case you dig a hole for yourself. What makes it worse for the Liverpool lads is so many of the pundits today have an Anfield background.

I have mentioned Tommy Smith and Phil Thompson elsewhere, but every Saturday night on *Match of the Day* you have Alan Hansen and Mark Lawrenson with a nationwide audience. Add Kenny, Kevin Keegan, Jan Molby, John Barnes, Ian St John, Ray Clemence, Nigel Spackman, Jim Beglin and David Fairclough, and Liverpool can field a complete team plus a couple of subs of ex-players who work in the media. Incidentally, I think big Al does the job with some style – he is the best of the lot – but my opinion may not be shared by the Liverpool individuals who are on the receiving end of his comments!

When Kenny was manager at Liverpool and Blackburn he never said much but nobody complained because he produced championship winning teams at both places. His problems began at Newcastle. He was following Kevin Keegan, who had the media eating out of his hand even though he was never as successful as Kenny when it came to winning trophies. In the end that seemed to be forgotten but you have to know Kenny to realise he could never change his ways just to improve his public image. You need to be strong to stick so rigidly to your principles the way he does but I admire him for that. He won't budge just for the sake of it and it has cost him some popularity contests along the way.

Not many get close to Kenny. I smile when I read some of the interviews he has given and the journalist tries to imply he has managed to describe the real Kenny Dalglish. Don't you believe it. It would take considerably more than one interview to get anywhere near understanding Kenny – and I am not referring to his accent either! I don't claim to know all about him even though we go back a long way.

Although many of us are becoming aware of the need to be more media-conscious, only a handful of real experts in this field spring to mind. I can see problems ahead for Alan Shearer if he moves into management. Take a tip from me, Alan. Start polishing up your performance now so you will be ready when it is time to stop playing. As the England captain, Alan is constantly in demand for interviews and whenever I see him on television I get the impression he is not comfortable and wants to get it over with as soon as possible. His answers are short and cryptic and his body language tells me he would rather be somewhere else. Maybe it is the way he is made but I can promise him once the adulation of being a great player has faded he will discover it is a different world in management – assuming he decides to take the plunge. He does not look at ease when there is a camera on him but in this day and age it is something we all have to live with.

In Portugal I dealt with an army of media men and it was far more intense than anything I experienced at Rangers or Liverpool. They say every match day is election day for the president, meaning any loss could immediately threaten his position and presumably the coach he employs.

If you are media-friendly it can give you some breathing space when times are tough. And an extra two or three months may be all it needs to turn a difficult situation around. Eventually they will come looking for you because that is the nature of the business. Ron Atkinson is an obvious example of how to be a success in this field. Throughout his career he has appreciated that he can have them on his side by being co-operative and giving them the soundbites they crave. Many years working in television has helped him because he understands what they need and he provides it. Full marks to him. He understands their business. He loves management so much he takes the setbacks in his stride and is always ready for another go when the call comes. After all these years he remains high-profile and totally at ease when there is a microphone or a tape recorder stuck in his face. He is a lesson to everyone. He is always smiling and giving the impression he enjoys it even when he may not be.

Terry Venables is another great example. When you are the England manager the pressure increases tenfold but Terry can charm the birds out of the trees and was probably the most popular man in that particular job. I think Graham Taylor, Bobby Robson and Glenn Hoddle would vouch for that. Kevin Keegan would also be on the list. They worshipped him on Tyneside even though he never won anything for Newcastle. That speaks volumes for the strength of his personality. He won them over and remains a big favourite with the Toon Army.

I don't think it is a coincidence that Ron, Terry and Kevin

have extensive experience of working on live television – when you have to be spot-on with what you say because there are no second takes. Make a gaffe and the nation hears it. The exception would be George Graham, who is rarely seen in a television studio. It took him time to adjust but after his ban from the game he returned stronger in every sense. He knows how to appear relaxed in front of a camera and although he never says anything wildly controversial he still manages to deliver exactly what he wants to say and he does it in a manner acceptable to the media. That is not as easy as it may sound. George is a clever and articulate man. Style is always the word I associate with George – he will appreciate that.

Others high on my list as good PR performers may surprise you. Look at Gordon Strachan and Martin O'Neill screaming and shouting – they almost come across as candidates for the funny farm. I remember bumping into Gordon at a match in Birmingham one evening and I advised him to start wearing a suit instead of a track suit and charging up and down like a dervish.

It may sound silly but it does affect your behaviour. When you are wearing trainers and a track suit it is too easy to allow your emotions to run away with you because you are so close to the action and you do feel involved. When a shirt, tie and jacket are the order of the day you do feel more inhibited and aware of the need to behave in more restrained fashion. I know because I used to be like Gordon and Martin. I told Gordon to be careful otherwise he might have to face the same operation I endured as Liverpool manager. He said he would try and I gather he only pops up in the dugout for the second half these days. Well, that's a good start, Gordon.

The same applies with Martin. You can see him kicking every ball for Leicester and he must feel as physically tired as his players when the final whistle goes. Yet when he and Gordon are interviewed on television just minutes after the game they look reasonably calm and certainly come across as intelligent, passionate men. I hope they can sleep at night because you do need to switch off from the game.

I have my own remedies. I enjoy a good bottle of red wine – strictly medicinal you understand – or I take my dogs for a brisk walk before I go to bed. It works for me but we are all different. Who knows? Expending all that energy at a game may work for Gordon and Martin. The way it was explained to me, there are two types of stress in soccer management. One guy can find sitting at home in his chair with his pipe and slippers relaxing whereas another doing exactly the same thing will be turning everything over in his mind and adding to the stress factor.

So why do we put ourselves through all this mental turmoil? The financial rewards can be considerable if you are a success but it goes deeper than that for most football people. You get hooked on the game. That is why there is never any shortage of candidates for managerial vacancies at all levels.

I took a year out and it was the best thing I ever did – but when the call came to return, I could not resist.

24

Fergie – Man of the Moment

Alex Ferguson's incredible achievements with Manchester United in the 1998–99 season have elevated him to the very top bracket of football managers. When you talk about the managerial greats of the game the list is surprisingly small. Jock Stein, Matt Busby, Bill Shankly, Bob Paisley and Brian Clough immediately spring to mind, and probably Sir Alf Ramsey for winning the World Cup for England. Ferguson is being rightly bracketed with that elite group after completing an unprecedented European Cup, FA Cup and League Championship treble for United.

Stein did the same in Scotland when Celtic became the first British club to win the European Cup back in 1967, and also claimed the Scottish Cup and the League Championship in the same season. A year later Sir Matt kept the coveted trophy in the UK when United beat Benfica at Wembley. Shanks is rightly credited with transforming Liverpool and laying the foundations for what was to follow as they dominated the club scene at home and abroad for so many years. He spent 15 seasons at Anfield, won three Championships, the club's first European trophy – the UEFA Cup in 1973 – plus two FA Cup competitions.

Bob's record at one club will probably stand for ever. It included three European Cups and five championships in an amazing haul of 16 trophies. I have talked about Bob in previous chapters and shall always be grateful to him for bringing me to Liverpool and providing me with the best days of my playing career. Brian Clough too deserves to be a member of this very exclusive club after winning two European Cups for Nottingham Forest, who with all due respect rarely get mentioned in the same breath as Celtic, Manchester United and Liverpool when Europe is the topic. That only serves to emphasise what a remarkable achievement it was for Clough to bring the top prize to Forest.

Ferguson is right up there with the very best and you can expect to be regaled with tales about him from all sorts of people who will claim to know the secret of his success. Well, I don't know him very well although we were rivals when he managed Aberdeen and I was at Rangers, and our paths crossed again when we both moved to England. It was when I was a player that Alex Ferguson made the biggest impression on me – he is the only manager who ever dropped me! And I am going right back to my schooldays in Edinburgh. Ever since I started playing football as a kid, working my way up through schools and youth teams, I preserved that proud record. It extended to my time at Middlesbrough, Liverpool, Sampdoria and the national team until we went to Mexico for the 1986 World Cup.

A dubious claim to fame? I don't think so, although it might provide a good question for your next pub quiz on football. I can remember the occasion vividly and it gave an indication of Fergie's skills as a manager. I never resented him for spoiling my record – in fact I agreed with his decision – but it was the way he explained his reasons which made the biggest impression on me. I know to my cost that you can be stuck with a reputation in this game which is not always complimentary. Alex has a few enemies out there who are quick to jump on him whenever they get the chance. If you believe everything you read he has a hot temper and is never backward at coming forward when he wants to get his point of view across. The FA, referees, rival managers – they all get a volley from time to time which portrays Alex as a hard man who is only concerned with promoting the interests of his own club. I don't see anything wrong with that. It is the way I operated when I was at Rangers. I was not trying to copy the Ferguson blueprint which first emerged when he was at Aberdeen but I was working along similar lines when I first entered management.

If that is the way Ferguson is regarded by the public I can assure you it bears little relation to the way he handles his players, if my experience is anything to go by. When we went to Mexico, Alex had taken charge of the Scottish team following the death of Jock Stein at a World Cup qualifying game in Cardiff. He did not want the job but he was the obvious choice. I was the captain and determined to be in the best shape of my life because I realised this would be my last chance to play at this level. The old fitness bug had struck again and because the games were being played at altitude I wanted to lose some weight before the tournament began. It can be very tiring and physically draining, playing football in those conditions but I was convinced my plan would suit me best when the games began. Maybe it was a mistake and when we started preparing at our base in New Mexico I was not feeling at my very best. I put that down to the altitude problem but I did myself no favours when we eventually arrived at our HQ for the first game. I ordered an omelette for my evening meal and while I and the rest of the team waited for the food to be served, a waiter produced some bread in a basket. I went to pick up a piece and noticed something on the bread. On closer examination it looked like bird or chicken droppings and that was enough to put me off eating Mexican food for the duration of the trip.

From then on I existed on Mars bars, bottled water and glucose drinks. I played poorly in the first game against Denmark but it was worse in the next match against West Germany. Gordon Strachan gave us the lead but we lost 2–1 and I was struggling at the end of the game. In fact it was the worst I have ever felt after a football match. We would be weighed after every game because the very good medical team with the Scottish squad were well aware of the dangers of weight loss playing at altitude and kept a close watch on all the players. The scales showed I had lost nearly two stone although I did not need them to confirm something I already knew. Just buckling my trousers told me: I was forced to tighten my belt to stop my pants falling down!

I knew I was not playing well and the thought had crossed my mind that it could cost me my place in the team for the next game, against Uruguay. I had my own room at the hotel, although it is something of an exaggeration to describe it as a room. It reminded me of a small cave. It had no windows and was very claustrophobic. Late one night I was lying in my bed when I heard footsteps on the tiled floor of the corridor. Call it instinct but I just knew it was Alex Ferguson on his way to tell me he was leaving me out for the Uruguay game. I had been playing the game for a long time and I was looking for signs that I could be left out. Perhaps it was a compliment to Alex's management skills but there were no indications it was going to happen until he knocked on my door to break the news to me personally.

I don't think he enjoyed doing it. He was sympathetic and almost uncomfortable as he explained his reasons. I am sure it was a difficult decision for him to take although I have to say if the roles had been reversed I would have done exactly the same thing. I can only presume he had been turning it over in his head for some time and that was why he left it so late on this particular evening to tell me I was out. He found it hard. He knew I had captained Scotland on many occasions and that this was my last World Cup. He explained why he was taking this step and I understood and had to agree with everything he said. If it is possible to break that type of news gently he succeeded. He was professional, compassionate and I respected him for taking the trouble to seek me out. I have not forgotten that episode and it gave me an insight into the way he handled management. It does not surprise me that he receives such loyalty from his players at Manchester United because I saw for myself how he dealt with difficult situations on that night in my airless cave.

It was a tough one for him because he knew Uruguay were a nasty, cynical team and if I had been fully fit he would have wanted somebody like me to face them. Instead Paul McStay, who was being groomed as my successor, took my place and we went out of the World Cup. It was my last game before I became a player-manager so Alex can claim to be the only manager who ever dropped me. I was in charge of my own destiny when I went to Rangers. Later, at a charity lunch in Glasgow which I attended, he apologised for that decision which again is a measure of the man.

You live or die by your decisions in this game and Alex has never ducked a major issue. He left Alan Hansen out for that World Cup when he was playing out of his skin for Liverpool

– and who else but Ferguson would change his goalkeeper for an FA Cup Final replay as he did when he dropped Jim Leighton and replaced him with Les Sealey? Big decisions taken by a big man. It was not all plain sailing for him when he became a manager but he really began to make people take notice when he turned Aberdeen into the best club side in Scotland. He broke the Rangers–Celtic stranglehold and won a European trophy while he was at Pittodrie. Some of the lessons he learned then he has used to his advantage at Manchester United. At Aberdeen he played on the provincial theme, the old chip-on-the-shoulder routine. He convinced the players that everybody in Glasgow was against them; he floated the idea that they would get no favours from referees when they played the big games and that the media was just waiting to shoot them down. That created a togetherness amongst his players and I did exactly the same at Rangers. Our fans had a song which went: 'No one likes us, we don't care' because I was also promoting the idea that everyone wanted to bring us down a peg or two. Just because we were the biggest club in Scotland was no reason why anyone else should receive preferential treatment when they played us was my argument.

Alex did the same at Old Trafford. They have the biggest fanbase in Britain and one which stretches all around the world. You either love them or hate them and he has used that to his advantage. Opinion is split right down the middle when it comes to Manchester United and Alex has been shrewd enough to exploit that as he almost swept the board in the 1998–99 season.

He is without question the top manager in British football today and I honestly believe he could go on to become the greatest the game has ever seen. I don't say that lightly, having worked for Bob Paisley and Jock Stein but he is capable of eclipsing everything they achieved. I remember the night Jock died. I was suspended for the game against Wales, and Scotland needed a point to make it to Mexico. At half time we were losing and after the team had gone back on to the pitch Jock, Alex and I remained in the dressing room. It was the first time I had ever seen the great man flustered. He turned to Alex and me and said, 'What should we do?' It was totally out of character for him to show any signs of uncertainty but we were not to know he was feeling ill and sadly he passed away that night at Ninian Park, as Scotland gained the point they needed to qualify for the Finals.

Manchester United are now the kings of English football and it is Alex Ferguson who has made them so. His planning, knowledge and ability has placed them in this position and they are capable of staying for several years. I know he had some difficult years at the start when he went to Old Trafford but their patience and belief in him has paid off. Just look at the age of his team. Some have yet to reach their peak even though they have accomplished so much. If he did not introduce any new faces they would still remain the dominant force and I am sure he has no intention of leaving the squad as it is. He needed a replacement for Peter Schmeichel and wasted no time in recruiting Aston Villa's Mark Bosnich. Ferguson himself shows no sign of retiring and why should he? The game is everything to him. He has assembled a group of players who play it the way he wants and they have reaped the rewards. He has the best squad in the country and it is no coincidence that they also work harder than anyone else. It reminds me of the great Liverpool years. Everybody wanted to play for them then but now ask any player worth his salt which club would be his first choice and there would be only one answer.

If I was a gambler I would put a few bob on Alex Ferguson becoming the most successful manager in the history of the game. You can't say more than that about the man.

25

Glasgow: Full Circle for Kenny

My enduring friendship with Kenny Dalglish hardly got off to the most auspicious of starts when we roomed together for the first time in 1974, but ever since, football has had a habit of linking our careers on and off the pitch.

We were team mates at club and international level when we both played for Liverpool and when I took the plunge into management at Rangers, Kenny was already in charge at Anfield. It is history now that I replaced him at Liverpool when he resigned, and now he is back at his beloved Celtic the wheel has turned full circle because he will be determined to match or surpass what Walter Smith and I achieved at Ibrox.

Football really is a small world when you compare our careers but neither of us was to know what was to follow after a distinctly uncomfortable introduction. The Scotland team manager in 1974 was Willie Ormond and he brought me into the squad for the first time for a game against West Germany in Frankfurt just before the World Cup was staged in that country. Quite by chance I was down to share a hotel room with Kenny but I hardly saw him on the entire trip. He never seemed to be around after we had finished training and he certainly kept some unusual hours for a professional footballer. He was up and about long after midnight and I did not know where he was. He certainly was not resting in our room and I found it all very confusing. He was already an established figure at this level, with a reputation as a model pro who was destined to become one of Scotland's biggest heroes.

That was not the impression I got after watching his behaviour in Frankfurt but I would have cringed with embarrassment if I had known what he thought of me at the time. Because it was my first trip representing my country I was determined to look the part and when we checked into our hotel I put my hair dryer, aftershave and deodorant in our bathroom. Kenny must have noted this but he did not say anything. After all, we hardly knew each other and it was not until years later that he admitted he suspected I might have been gay! He would not enter our room until he was certain I was fast asleep just in case his worst fears were confirmed! Now, we are entirely different types but we were never that different.

That was how our friendship began and it could only improve after that. We were room mates for seven years with Scotland and Liverpool and we quickly slipped into a routine which suited both of us. The drill was if anyone knocked at the door he would answer it and I would take responsibility for ordering room service because nobody could understand Kenny's broad Glaswegian accent when he picked up the telephone.

The night before a game he would always take a sleeping tablet and I became accustomed to waking up in the early hours to hear him talking to himself. He would think he was having a conversation with me but I would just grunt, say goodnight and drop off again and that seemed to be all he required. A relatively painless exercise and infinitely more agreeable than acting as his straight man when he practised his one-line jokes on me before testing them on a wider audience. I was his stooge and he would judge my reaction before introducing his gags to the rest of the squad. I like to think I spared them from some of the worst jokes in his repertoire. If they cringed at some that did escape into the public domain they should have heard some of the offerings I rejected when we were on our own!

Only really close friends can have fierce arguments secure in the knowledge that it won't damage the relationship and Kenny and I would fight like cats and dogs on occasions because we both wanted to be winners. He was the team shop steward. I lost count of the rows we had in private and there were more public occasions when we came close to blows. I can remember games for Liverpool against Coventry and Fulham when it was all going wrong and we engaged in heated exchanges on the pitch which forced other members of the team to keep us apart just in case it all went out of control. That was the way we were when there was a game to be won. But if anyone on the opposing side tried to take liberties with Kenny they had to be prepared to deal with me as well because I was always ready to be by his side. He could look after himself but a little moral support did not go to waste when you had my reputation.

It won't surprise anyone when I nominate Kenny as the best player I ever saw but he also helped me in other ways. He married young when I was still a bit of a Jack the lad and he pointed me in the right direction when it came to behaving in a professional manner. We are completely different types but I quickly came under his influence. He was staying at the old Holiday Inn in Liverpool with his wife, Marina, and I moved in there when I joined the club so it was inevitable we saw a lot of each other right from the beginning of my time at Liverpool.

It is strange how events unfold in football and although Rangers will always be my first love in Scotland, they can expect a stronger challenge to their position now Kenny is back in Glasgow. I believe his arrival will stimulate both clubs and help to raise the standard of the game in Scotland. Ideally you would like to see a couple of other clubs in a position to offer a stern challenge but it is unlikely to happen because Rangers and Celtic have the resources and support to outstrip everyone else.

Kenny's appointment will have been noted at Ibrox. They will know his name and reputation will help to attract big-name players to Parkhead and another Old Firm battle for supremacy is about to begin. Celtic were the undisputed kings before Walter and I went to Rangers and now Kenny's brief will be to restore them at the expense of my old club. It is interesting how the club is being structured, with Kenny directing operations and John Barnes as the coach. He always had an opinion on the game as a player and was never slow to voice it and now he has the opportunity to put his ideas into practice. Some have mocked the appointment of Terry McDermott with the title of social manager, but I can understand why Kenny wants him on board.

We called Terry the Pied Piper when we were all together at Anfield because we followed wherever he suggested if we were having a night out. He is a lively, humorous guy with a great personality and he is guaranteed to bring a smile to the dressing room. With Kenny pointing everyone in the right direction I can see the new set-up at Celtic being a success. And, by going home, Kenny will also be able to improve his golf handicap by taking his pick of the fine courses close to the city!

I am sure it will all make for a particularly exciting period in Scotland because Rangers won't sit back and allow anyone to steal their thunder. David Murray, the chairman, is as ambitious and aggressive as he ever was and will be determined to build on recent success. But he has already seen the impact of Kenny's arrival with the signing of Eyal Berkovic, the Israeli star I first introduced to English football at Southampton.

Eyal is one of the best I have ever worked with and I am confident he will become a major performer in Scotland. He is not the biggest, but he is sharp and cute, and defenders will find him very elusive when they try to tackle him. You would think he had eyes in the back of his head when he skips away from trouble. He reminds me of the American basketball stars who wrong-foot the opposition by looking one way and throwing the ball in the other direction. Berkovic has the ability to do that with his passing and it is very difficult for anyone to anticipate what he will do when he is in possession of the ball. He does not have the physique to fight and scrap with people but in his own way he is an aggressive type of player and his touch and control will enable him to avoid any potential traps. He is destined to be a big success in Scotland.

Kenny will appreciate his vision and intelligence on the pitch because those were some of the qualities that made him such a great player. I have already warned David Murray that Celtic will be a bigger danger now Kenny is at the helm but the overall winners should be football fans. Kenny will raise the standards at Celtic, Rangers will certainly respond, and the Old Firm rivalry is set to become more intense than ever.

26

Glasgow: How Times Have Changed

I was back in Glasgow in May 1999 working for Sky TV at the Scottish FA Cup Final. It was only the second time I had seen Rangers in a competitive game since I left in 1991 and it made me realise how much things had changed in that time.

For a start there is the new-look Hampden Park which has been rebuilt and is now a magnificent stadium which stands comparison with the best in Europe. That can only help the international team because they now have a home to be proud of. When I was at Rangers I used Ibrox Park as one of my big selling points when I was persuading the top English players to move north. Since those days Celtic have refurbished their ground at Parkhead and Scotland can now boast three international-class stadia.

I could not resist a smile when the Celtic and Rangers teams came out of the tunnel before the game. They only had six Scots between them – and one of those was an adopted Jock in Jonathan Gould, the son of the former Welsh manager. I was working as a match summariser alongside Charlie Nicholas and I had to admit on air that I did not know too much about some of the foreign players in the Celtic side. Everyone has heard about Andre Kanchelskis, Lorenzo Amoruso and Sergio Porrini but apart from Henrik Larsson I had not seen the other foreign imports in the Celtic team.

I knew they were international players in their own right but with all due respect to them they were not household names. That is the difference between the two clubs right now. Rangers boast the star attractions and Celtic will need to loosen the purse strings and spend serious money if they are to keep pace with their rivals. I can remember the misgivings expressed when I proposed to recruit English players to build my Rangers team, and all hell broke loose when Maurice Johnston became the first Catholic player at Ibrox. Thank goodness minds have been opened since those days. Now Rangers recruit from all over the world and nobody questions the religious beliefs of their Italian imports. As long as they do the business on the field every-one is happy, and that is the way it should be.

When I was their manager I never had an open cheque book but now Rangers can compete with any club for the very best talent anywhere in the world. In the mid-1990s the very idea that Rangers would boast players from South America as well as Europe would have been laughed at. And to suggest they could earn twice as much money in Scotland would also be dismissed as a fairy tale. Yet that is the reality today and a measure of how far Rangers have progressed.

Some things have not changed. The incident which led to the resignation of Donald Findlay after the Cup Final high-lights the fact that the sectarian issue remains a problem. I know it is difficult for people with little or no knowledge of Glasgow to understand how an intelligent man like Donald

Findlay could allow himself to become a central figure when he was caught singing Rangers songs – which by tradition are anti-Catholic. The vice-chairman of the club and an eminent barrister – you may argue he is the last person who should become embroiled in such sensitive matters. But this was a victory party to celebrate a Rangers triumph over their arch-rivals and whether people like it or not this is the way it is in the west of Scotland.

It was not unusual at Rangers–Celtic games to see lawyers or doctors seated in the directors' box at Ibrox or Parkhead arguing for the full 90 minutes of an Old Firm contest and barely taking any notice of what was happening on the pitch. It has been that way for 100 years and it may take another century before it is finally put to rest. It may not even happen then. There have been some significant changes on that front and I believe a more tolerant attitude is beginning to prevail but both clubs know in their hearts that it will never go away completely. In England when Liverpool play Everton or Arsenal meet Spurs the rivalry between the players ends with the final whistle but that does not apply in Scotland. It is rare for the players to mix after an Old Firm confrontation and I know the English players I brought to Ibrox found that difficult to understand. They were accustomed to having a drink with the opposition once the game was over but that was not the case when Rangers played Celtic.

Coming from Edinburgh, I was never caught up in the great religious debate. Hearts and Hibs are the big rivals in the capital but it is all small beer compared to what happens in Glasgow. When I was a boy I walked a mile to school every day with Peter Marinello who went on to play for Hibs and Arsenal. We grew up together. He is a Catholic and I am a Protestant but it did not mean anything to either of us. I went to Broomhouse Primary and he was a pupil at St Joseph's. The two schools shared the same playing fields and played each other at football without a problem. The nearest we came to violence was snowball fights in the winter!